Sacram

of

Unity

Sacrament

of

Unity

THE EUCHARIST AND THE CHURCH

Walter Cardinal Kasper

Translated by Brian McNeil

A Herder & Herder Book
The Crossroad Publishing Company
New York

Original publication: *Sakrament der Einheit. Eucharistie und Kirche*
Herder Verlag, Freiburg, Basle, and Vienna, 2004.
The Crossroad Publishing Company
481 Eighth Avenue, New York, NY 10001

This book is set in 13/17 Centaur.
The display type is Bodoni Antiqua.

Printed in the United States of America

Library of Congress Cataloging-in-Publication Data

Kasper, Walter, 1933-
    [Sakrament der Einheit. English]
    Sacrament of unity : the Eucharist and the church / Walter
Kasper ; translated by Brian McNeil.
      p. cm.
    Includes bibliographical references and index.
    ISBN 0-8245-2314-8 (alk. paper)
    1. Lord's Supper—Catholic Church. 2. Catholic Church—
Doctrines. I. Title.
    BX2230.3.K3713 2004
    234'.163—dc22
                          2004023881

1 2 3 4 5 6 7 8 9 10 08 07 06 05 04

*Dedicated to the many parish communities
of the diocese of Rottenburg-Stuttgart
with whom I had the privilege
of celebrating the Eucharist
during the ten years
of my ministry
as bishop there*

Contents

Preface

The world in which we live is not a place of unshattered calm. The reality in which we live is characterized by conflicts, where unity is impaired and broken, and this reality cries out for healing and reconciliation.

The biblical texts emphasize the connection between Eucharist and unity, Eucharist and church. The fact that fidelity to the truth makes it impossible in today's situation for all Christians to meet around the one table of the Lord and take part in the one Supper of the Lord is a deep wound inflicted on the Body of the Lord. Ultimately, it is scandalous.

On the feast of Corpus Christi in 2004, Pope John Paul II announced that a Eucharistic Year, which will have the Eucharist as its theme, would be held, beginning with the Eucharistic World Congress in Mexico City in October 2004 and ending with the World Synod of Bishops in October 2005.

The publication of this book, at the very beginning of the Eucharistic Year, is meant as an initial theological and pastoral aid. We shall explore the topic that the pope has proposed for the Eucharistic Year: the essential connection between Eucharist and church, both in the personal life of the individual Christian and in the life of the church as a whole.

I begin with an essay on the significance of the Eucharist for the worshiping life of parishes; this is based on my experiences as bishop of the diocese of Rottenburg-Stuttgart and takes up the open questions with which we are confronted at the present time.

The second and third chapters are biblically orientated reflections on essential aspects of the Eucharist. The fourth chapter is based on an address delivered at the National Catholic Assembly ("Katholikentag") in Ulm in 2004 and situates the ecumenical aspects of the Eucharist in the broader context of an "ecumenism of life." Ecumenically speaking, we are at an intermediary stage, in a period of transition. Happily, we have reached a number of milestones along our way; but we have not yet reached our goal. Ecumenism is a process whereby life grows. On this path of growing and maturing, many intermediary steps are required. These are meant to lead finally to fellowship in the Eucharist—the sacrament of unity.

The fifth and sixth chapters in this book—an essay reflecting at a fundamental theological level on the wealth of perspectives of the Eucharist and my address at the Eucharistic Congress in October 2004—seek to help the reader grasp more profoundly the theological issues involved here.

The pope sees the Eucharistic Year as lying at the very heart of the pastoral perspectives that he formulated on the threshold of the third millennium in his apostolic letter *Novo millennio ineunte* (2001): "To know Christ!" and "To start afresh from Christ!" There is a profound and inherent link between this program and the Eucharist, since the latter is the most concentrated form of Christ's presence among us.

As the encyclical *Ecclesia de eucharistia* (2003) has reminded us anew, the Eucharist is the source, the center, and the summit both of the Christian's life and of the life of the church—and hence also of the pastoral work that the church carries out. In the church's mission, her task is always to become in a convincing manner what she already is, in terms of her essential nature: as it were a "sacrament," that is, a sign and instrument of unity and of peace in the world (LG 1). The Eucharist is the sacrament of this unity.

I am happy to dedicate this book to the many parish communities of the diocese of Rottenburg-Stuttgart with whom I was privileged to celebrate the Eucharist during the ten years of my ministry as bishop there.

WALTER CARDINAL KASPER
Rome
29 June 2004
Feast of Saints Peter and Paul

The Celebration of the Eucharist and the Worshiping Life of the Parish Communities

Open Questions–Necessary Answers

The celebration of the Eucharist is the source and summit of the life of our church and of each individual parish community (cf. LG 11). It is the great bequest of the Lord, which he left to us on the eve of his suffering and death (Luke 22:19f.). It is the most precious of all the treasures that we—as church—possess. It is the heart of our church. Everything else tends toward the Eucharist, and from it goes forth the power that imparts vigor to every other sphere of church life—and not least the power we need in our own personal life. This is why virtually everything in pastoral work depends on the correct understanding and praxis of the eucharistic celebration, and why we can never do enough in our endeavor to attain a deeper comprehension and a worthy realization of this "mystery of faith."

Open Questions

I am aware of the great efforts made by priests and dea-
cons, by their full-time collaborators in pastoral activity, and by so many persons who carry out the various
liturgical ministries to ensure a worthy celebration of
the Eucharist in our parishes. We owe a particular debt
of gratitude to all those who bear responsibility for the
correct celebration of the liturgy, and especially of the
Eucharist. We must acquire an ever-profounder understanding of the liturgy and allow it to bear fruit in our
life. This will make our own joy in the celebration of
the Eucharist contagious.

Nevertheless, a number of grave problems demand
our attention. In recent years, the number of those par-
ticipating in Sunday Mass has declined and our
churches have become emptier on normal Sundays.
Many of those who do come to church have a dimin-
ishing understanding of the liturgical texts and symbols; many have virtually lost their grasp on the truth
that the Eucharist is a sacred action in which "the work
of our redemption" is carried out (SC 2). Young people in particular find the language and the forms of the
liturgy inaccessible. And we all suffer under the fact
that declining numbers of priests make it no longer
possible to celebrate the Eucharist each Sunday in every
Catholic parish in Germany. In my eyes, this is not just

a minor problem. It affects the very heart of things and is an acute ecclesial emergency.[1]

Above all, I wish to help us achieve a deeper understanding of the Eucharist, for it is only when we ourselves grasp in our heart and with our mind what is going on in this "mystery of faith" that we will be able to hand on our faith in a convincing way and to find the correct forms for the celebration of the Eucharist.[2]

Discovering the Liturgy Afresh and Promoting Its Understanding

We are told of the earliest community in Jerusalem: "They partook of food with glad and generous hearts" (Acts 2:46). From the apostolic beginnings of our church onward, Christians have gathered on Sunday to celebrate the Eucharist. From the very outset, the celebration of Sunday, the day of the Lord, and the celebration of the Eucharist, the Supper of the Lord, have been inseparably linked. Together, they form the heart and the special characteristic of a Christian life. From the earliest period of our church comes the following definition of what it means to be a Christian: "living in accordance with Sunday." And the martyrs in that early age said: "We cannot live without celebrating the day of the Lord."

Celebrating divine worship means interrupting the hectic rushing around and the humdrum routine of our daily living in order to reflect on what is essential for our life, what provides us with support and sustenance. When we celebrate the Eucharist on Sunday, we become aware of the source and the goal of our life: we do not live of our own selves, nor do we live for our own selves. Every Sunday, we come together in order to praise the goodness of God, which is the source of our life and which we experience day by day. And we thank God for giving us Jesus Christ as the way, the truth, and the life (John 14:6). Every Sunday is a "little Easter day," for in the eucharistic celebration, we recall God's central salvific deed, namely, the death and resurrection of Jesus Christ, which become present in the Mass as the basis and the source of our hope. And finally, Jesus Christ himself is present in the Eucharist as spiritual nourishment both for this life and for life everlasting.

When we celebrate divine worship, this ought not to be a stiff and gloomy affair. Rather, the celebration should be joyful and alive. All who take part—children and young people, just as much as adults and the elderly—should be involved with heart and mind and with all their senses. Joy in God is our strength (Neh 8:10), and this means that we should celebrate the liturgy with as much solemnity as possible and in the presence of the entire parish community.

We must, however, note that worship must remain worship: it must not be turned into an "event." This is why it is wrong to evaluate the liturgy in terms of its entertainment value. On the contrary, the celebration of worship should be permeated by reverence for the God, who is holy, and reverence for the presence of our Lord in the sacrament. There must be a place for silence, reflection, adoration, and the personal encounter with God.

We call worship a "service," but not in the sense in which that word is used by the law of supply and demand: it is not a "service" orientated to the needs or desires of particular "target groups" which marketing research identifies. We may not turn it into an instrument for the interests, ideas, and pet topics that we or others may happen to have, nor may we misuse it as a vehicle for messages that we ourselves want to put across. The liturgy is never a means to an end: it is an end in itself. It is precisely by glorifying God that the liturgy serves the salvation of the human person.

Our present situation obliges us to discover anew the meaning of worship and to help ourselves understand it afresh. We spend a great deal of energy debating individual questions about how we should celebrate the liturgy, but *this* seems to me more important than all such issues. The primary task here is liturgical education, which is necessary both for all who work in pastoral ministry, and for the parish communities themselves. Mystagogy—the interpretation and explanation of the liturgical texts, symbols, and celebrations—can and should occur in a variety of contexts, in homilies, in series of thematic sermons, in parish catechesis, in religious education classes in school, and in public lectures.[3] I am convinced that this kind of liturgical formation, which penetrates the depths not only of the mind but also of the heart, can prove much more effective than short-term strategies to cope with specific issues. These always risk remaining on the surface of things and failing to see the essential point.

The Fundamental Significance of the Sunday Celebration of the Eucharist

From the very start, the Christian life and the life of the church have been linked to participation in the celebration of Sunday Mass. As Christians, we have been baptized into the death and resurrection of Jesus (Rom 6:3-11), and his cross and resurrection become present in the celebration of the Eucharist. Thus, our obligation as baptized persons to take part in Sunday Mass comes from the very depths of what it means for us to be Christians. The Sunday obligation (Code of Canon Law, 1247) is the external expression of this internal obligation. Naturally, there may be appropriate reasons which excuse one from participation in the Sunday Eucharist.[4] If, however, one has no adequate reason for staying away, but simply refuses to take part in the Mass out of an attitude of indifference, this is not something that can simply be shrugged off: for one is withholding oneself from God and from the parish community and refusing God's mighty offer of salvation.

Given the central significance of the Eucharist, the fact that it is no longer possible to celebrate Mass every Sunday in every parish affects the very heart of what it means for us to be Christians and to be the church. There is no simple and straightforward solution to this problem, and we must take care to avoid false solutions that would obscure the central significance of the Eucharist.

Although in many cases there is no alternative to holding a celebration of the Word of God on Sunday instead of the Eucharist,[5] this can never be anything other than an emergency solution. The exception may never be permitted to become the normal case to which we get accustomed. We may not "make a virtue of necessity" and claim that this is *the* solution that points the way to the future, for that would be possible only if we were to abandon our identity as church and as Catholics. Before we adopt this solution, we must exhaust all other possibilities, for only so will we remain faithful to the bequest of the Lord and to the apostolic tradition of our church.

Naturally, it is equally inappropriate to propose as a solution that the individual priest should celebrate ever more and more Masses. The celebration of the Eucharist must remain a high point for the priest himself too, and there is, in fact, a limit to the number of times one can celebrate a high point. This means that the stipulation in canon law that a priest may not celebrate Mass on Sundays and holy days more than three times (canon 905 §2) makes good sense, and I ask parishes to respect this and not to make excessive physical and spiritual demands of their priests.

How are we to ensure that as many parishes as possible can celebrate the Eucharist on Sundays, despite the declining numbers of priests? Here, parishes must demonstrate solidarity: it is not acceptable that more than one Mass should be celebrated in some parishes on Sunday, while others must do without the Eucharist. This applies with particular force to cities with a number of parishes: here, it is often the case that too many Eucharists are celebrated. The early Christian practice, which remains in force in the Eastern churches up to the present day and was observed in the Catholic Church until well into the nineteenth century, was that only *one* Eucharist should be celebrated in each community (or in each church) as *the* assembly of the community. The present situation should cause us to reflect anew on this tradition and to repristinate it in keeping with our own circumstances. Our pastoral goal must be to make the celebration of the Eucharist a real possibility in as many parishes as possible.

This also requires solidarity among priests. In many instances, one priest looks after only one parish; indeed, there are places where several priests reside, so that each of them celebrates only one liturgy. At the same time, however, other priests have the burden of holding a large number of services; yet even so, they often find themselves unable to celebrate the Eucharist in *all* the communities entrusted to their care. Here, groups of parishes and deaneries must achieve a proper balance with regard to the number and the times of the services. As priests, we do not bear responsibility only for our own particular parish or our own sector of pastoral work (such as a hospital). We share responsibility for the church as a whole.

It has unfortunately become common in many places to speak of a priest being "flown in" to help out by celebrating Mass. This absurd image betrays a false understanding both of the Eucharist and of the community. One cannot view the celebration of the Eucharist and of the other sacraments as an expression on an elevated cultic plane of human relationships! God's salvation never comes from ourselves—from the individual

Christian or from the community. It always comes "from outside" and "from above." As I shall show below, this principle finds sacramental and symbolic expression in priestly ordination and in the fact that the priestly ministry is absolutely necessary, if the Eucharist is to be celebrated.

We must also bear in mind that a single parish is never a unit that exists of and for its own self. It lives in, and on the basis of, its fellowship with all the other parish communities, with the local church (or diocese), and with the worldwide church. A priest who comes from outside the parish to celebrate Mass can help people become aware of this Catholic breadth by showing them something of the church that lies beyond their own parish borders. Such a priest may come often, or even on a regular basis; or he may come only once, and will be presented to the community at the beginning of the service. In either case, he is not an outsider—even on human terms. For there ought to be no "outsiders" in the church, no "foreigners," but only brothers and sisters in Christ!

All the Baptized Are Called to Active Participation in the Eucharist

The one and only high priest is Jesus Christ himself, and it is he who is the real celebrant of the Eucharist.

In its celebration, he is present through the Holy Spirit in a variety of ways: in his Word, under the appearances of bread and wine, in the person of the priest, and in the celebrating community itself (cf. SC 7). The Second Vatican Council recalled the doctrine of the common priesthood of all the baptized and confirmed, and invited all the baptized who are present at the Eucharist to a conscious, pious, and active participation (SC 48; cf. 11; 14; 50). I myself am deeply committed to promoting this conscious, pious, and active participation of all Christians in the celebration of the liturgy.

Active participation is not to be misunderstood in a merely external sense, as if it entailed performing a large number of activities: it is expressed above all in praying and singing in common. Nevertheless, it is just as important that the tasks in the celebration of the Eucharist be distributed as widely as possible. The principal ministries open to the laity on the basis of their Baptism and confirmation include the tasks of lector and cantor, of leading the community in the prayers of the faithful, of serving at the altar, of singing in the choir, and of sacristan. All these persons are exercising a genuinely liturgical ministry (SC 29), and they deserve our gratitude and appreciation. They are not a "substitute" for priests who do not happen to be there. Rather, their ministry is a genuine expression of the dignity and mission conferred on them in Baptism and

in confirmation, and it enriches the worshiping life of
the parish.

The Indispensable Ministry of the Priest

Jesus did not call the people as a whole. In a special
way, he called the twelve and sent them out, and it was
to them that he entrusted the celebration of his Supper: "Do this in memory of me" (Luke 22:19; I Cor
11:24f.). After his resurrection, he chose particular
men and sent them out as apostles. From the very earliest times, in virtue of their ordination, the ministry of
presiding at the celebration of the Eucharist has been
the task of these men and of those whom they installed
as their successors by the laying-on of hands.

Neither the priestly ministry nor the Eucharist can
be thought of as derived "from below," as something
generated from within the community itself. The
Eucharist is rooted in the antecedent quality of God's
salvific action in the cross and the resurrection, and it
is the fulfilled sign of the abiding love with which God
comes down to us in Jesus Christ. This "antecedent"
character and this coming of salvation to us "from outside" and "from above" find their sacramental and symbolic expression in the mission of the priest in the
parish and in his relation vis-à-vis the community. It is,

of course, true that the priest, like every other Christian who receives salvation, is in the community; like everyone else, he needs to receive God's forgiveness and mercy, his help and his grace every day. In his priestly ministry, however, he stands over against the community as representative of the one who is the head of the church and the real celebrant, of him who issues the invitation and welcomes the guests to his Eucharist. This tension between being "in" the community and standing "over against" it is a fundamental dimension both of the priestly ministry itself and of the communal existence of the community. A priestless community is a self-contradiction, and a celebration of the Eucharist without the ministry of the priest is an impossibility.

Accordingly, the ministry of the priest is constitutive of the celebration of the Eucharist. This is true even in situations of extreme emergency. We hear of situations of terrible persecution in which no priest was available for years or even decades; but we never hear of communities or individual groups that celebrated the Eucharist without a priest. The only substitute for a priest is another priest, and if this was true in grave persecutions, it applies all the more strongly to our own situation of a—merely relative—shortage of priests.

This is why I accord high priority to the promotion of vocations, especially of vocations to the priesthood.

I ask everyone to contribute to this: young people, parents, teachers, the parishes, and, above all, priests themselves through their example and through their words of encouragement. The most important contribution is made by those who accept Jesus' command to ask the Lord to send out laborers into his harvest (Matt 9:38) and who pray for vocations. We are grateful for all that is done by the diocesan and pontifical commissions for the promotion of vocations. The Second Vatican Council expressed its confidence that the Lord would not abandon his church but would give her in future years a sufficient number of priests, provided that she prays for this (PO 16).

Laypeople as Collaborators in the Priestly Ministry

Since we have fewer priests today than in the past, many dioceses have made use of the possibilities opened up by the council and by postconciliar canon law to call suitably prepared laypersons and give them a special commission on the part of the bishop to share in carrying out particular tasks of the priestly ministry.[6] We are not speaking here of the wide field of tasks that laypersons carry out in the church and in the world in virtue of their Baptism and confirmation, and for which no extra commission is given, but of an exceptional commissioning to take part in tasks that belong properly to the priest. These commissions too have their sacramental root in Baptism and confirmation.

They include many tasks carried out by men and women collaborators in the pastoral work on a full-time, stipendiary basis; they also include nonstipendiary ministers such as those who help distribute Holy Communion during the Mass and those who lead celebrations of the Word of God in the absence of a priest. During my time as bishop of the diocese of Rottenburg-Stuttgart, I greatly esteemed the ministries that so many men and women carried out, and I have always been profoundly grateful to them for their commitment. I wish to encourage them to go on carrying out this service, which will continue to be vitally necessary in future years too.

As bishop of Rottenburg-Stuttgart, I insisted on the importance of cooperative pastoral work, that is, a system with binding directives governing the cooperation between the parish priest, as leader of the community, the full-time and nonstipendiary pastoral workers, and the parish council.[7] However, this cooperative style of pastoral work can be sustained in the long term only if the various pastoral ministries avoid all traces of mutual competition: each must have its own clear profile, while acknowledging and esteeming all the other forms of service. All of these ministries are equal in value, but they are not simply equal. If all those involved in one pastoral field try to do more or less the same things—although the ministers are not in fact equal—this can only lead to conflicts. If cooperative pastoral work is to be maintained in the longer term, we need to clarify both the profile of each individual ministry and the specific identity of the full-time and non-stipendiary pastoral and liturgical ministries.

The Ministry of Preaching in the Liturgy

The celebration of the liturgy is accomplished both verbally and by means of symbolic actions. Accordingly, it is not only the prayers—and especially the canon of the Mass—that form an essential and constitutive part of the celebration of the Eucharist. The same is true of the readings from sacred scripture and the explanation of these passages and of the liturgical texts themselves in the homily. The Second Vatican Council clearly expressed the importance of the proclamation of the Word of God and affirmed emphatically that preaching is the first task of the priest (see PO 4). The council does not see the priest only as the one who administers the sacrament when the Eucharist is celebrated, still less merely as the one who has the power to speak the words of consecration validly. The council sees him as the one who, before he gives the faithful the eucharistic bread of life, addresses God's Word to them as nourishment, strengthening, encouragement, consolation, and orientation for their lives, thereby preparing them for the salvific reception of the sacrament of the altar.

There is thus an intimate and indissoluble link between that part of the Eucharist which we call the liturgy of the Word and that part which is sacramental in the stricter sense of that term (SC 56). This in turn means that the homily is an integral part of the Eucharist (SC 52). It is the task of the one who presides at the Eucharist by virtue of his priestly ordination or of the one who has a prominent position in the community by virtue of his ordination to the diaconate. Accordingly, the canon law of the universal church prescribes that the homily in the Mass is reserved to the priest and the deacon (canon 767 §I).

This prescription of church law can appeal to a long tradition going back to the second century, a tradition also found in the confessional documents of the Reformation.[8]

I know that many priests justifiably complain that they are overburdened with work and sometimes cannot see how they are to cope with it all—especially when they have been entrusted with several parishes or when their health is not good. I have no simple solution to offer here, but I wish to make one point of fundamental importance: the only path to a solution is serious reflection on the priorities in our pastoral work. In this context, the New Testament gives a significant pointer, when the Acts of the Apostles make it clear that overwork is not a modern problem. The first apostles themselves had this problem, which indeed seems inherently linked to the apostolic task. When the apostles in the earliest community could not cope with the work expected of them, they said: "It is not right that we should give up preaching the Word of God to serve tables." Then they chose the "seven" for this diaconal work, adding: "But we will devote ourselves to prayer and to the ministry of the Word" (Acts 6:2-4). Paul too, who complains just as strongly about excessive burdens (2 Cor 11:28), sees the preaching of the gospel as his primary task (1 Cor 1:17). This means that sharing the load with others is both necessary and legitimate; it is necessary here to keep in view the priority of the task of preaching, which—all the more so, in today's situation!—is the primary and basic task of a priest.

Naturally, circumstances arise in which the priest can be justifiably excused from delivering the homily. In such cases, it is appropriate for a specially commissioned layperson to address some spiritual words to the community—an address that ought to be distinguishable from a homily in the strict sense. We must also reflect in depth on how lay theologians can contribute their competence to the life of the church in the future. Apart from the homily in the celebration of the Eucharist, there are many possibilities for laypersons (above all for those engaged in full-time pastoral ministry) to participate in the church's task of proclamation, both within and outside the liturgy.[9]

The Significance of Celebrations of the Word of God

It would be wrong to leave the church locked and empty in those parishes where it is not possible to celebrate the Eucharist on Sunday. I therefore recommend that the community should assemble on Sunday, even when no Mass can be celebrated. It is desirable that they come together to hear the Word of God, to pray and sing together, and thus to be strengthened in faith, hope, and love, and to experience the fellowship of other believers.[10] In these celebrations of the Word of God, Jesus Christ is present in his Word. In a parish where no Eucharist is celebrated in the local church, those who attend such a celebration fulfill the intention of the Sunday precept (cf. canon 1248 §2). The men and women who lead these celebrations are nominated

by the parish priest and the parish council and are commissioned by the bishop to carry out this ministry,
after receiving an appropriate training. Since these
liturgies of the Word are public acts of the church's
worship, ecclesiastical discipline must be observed.
Care must be taken not to hold these services in such a
way that they might be confused with the celebration of
the Mass. They must not give the impression of being
a "scaled-down Mass."

The liturgy of the Word on Sunday is valuable and
contributes to people's salvation; but although it is
highly recommended, it is in principle not an alternative nor a genuine substitute for the celebration of the
Eucharist. Accordingly, celebrations of the Word of
God on Sundays should not "compete" with a Mass
held in the same church. If one Mass is, in fact, celebrated on Sunday in a church, we should not offer a
liturgy of the Word in replacement of a second Mass
which cannot be held. It is, however, meaningful and
desirable to celebrate Lauds and Vespers (morning and
evening prayer) or an act of eucharistic worship on
Sunday in addition to the Mass (cf. SC 100); it is
important that we promote the celebration of the
Liturgy of the Hours in our parishes. It would be a real
impoverishment if the Eucharist were to become virtually the only form of worship ever experienced in a
parish, for then it would no longer be the high point.

The Celebration of Worship on Weekdays

The celebration of the Sunday Eucharist must be located within what we might call a garland of services on weekdays too. I believe that the most important point is the celebration of the Eucharist on weekdays. The simpler form gives it a meditative character. Every parish has people who feel the spiritual desire for the Mass even on weekdays, and we must not disappoint them or abandon them. Even if normally only a small group of believers come together for the celebration of weekday Mass, they symbolize and represent the entire community. And even for those who cannot take part, or do not wish to, there is a profound symbolic significance in the fact that bells ring for worship on weekdays too, and that the church does not remain locked and empty but is the place where God is worshiped. This too is a highly significant mode of the church's presence in people's everyday lives.

I am convinced that the praxis of daily celebration of the Eucharist is particularly important for the spiritual lives of us priests (see PO 18), since priestly existence is ultimately a eucharistic existence. Just as Christians cannot exist on the day of the Lord without the Supper of the Lord, so too we priests cannot exist without the regular—and normally, the daily—celebration of

Mass. If we celebrate it only "as required by other people's needs," we must ask where the heart of our existence lies, where we find the support necessary for our lives. This is why we must reflect anew on daily Mass; many must rediscover it and begin to practice it. I believe that this is an urgent need.

Solemnities and feasts, especially if they once were public holidays, ought to be marked with a solemn celebration of the Eucharist in the evening. Here I have in mind feasts such as the Presentation of the Lord (Candlemas) on February 2, Ash Wednesday, the feast of St. Joseph on March 19, the feast of the Annunciation of the Lord on March 25, the solemnity of the apostles Peter and Paul on June 29, the solemnity of the Assumption of Our Lady on August 15, All Souls Day on November 2, and the solemnity of the Immaculate Conception of Mary, the Virgin Mother of God, on December 8.

Even in those parishes where the daily celebration of the Eucharist is not possible, there ought to be some kind of daily liturgy of the Word or prayer in common: Lauds, Vespers, Compline, devotional services, eucharistic adoration, the rosary, Stations of the Cross, prayers in the early morning or late at night. The Eucharist ought in fact not be the only form of service in a parish. I believe it is important to take up anew all the variety and richness of our worship services. In many cases, a well-prepared liturgy of the Word may be more appropriate to the level of the faith of those taking part than the celebration of the Eucharist—for example, in occasional services such as weddings, school worship assemblies, or the jubilees or annual services of associations and groups.

The Celebration of the Eucharist
as the Church's Celebration

We do not celebrate the Eucharist alone, nor do we celebrate it privately: it is the praise, thanksgiving, sacrifice, and meal of the assembled people of God in each specific place, and it unites us to all the other communities that celebrate the Eucharist throughout the whole world. In particular, we celebrate each Eucharist in fellowship with the pope, who is the visible center of the church's unity, and with the bishop, who has the task of promoting unity in his diocese. In the Eucharist, the church becomes present as the one, holy, catholic, and apostolic church.

This fellowship reaches beyond this world and beyond this life, linking the living and the dead. It reaches into the great fellowship of the saints and into the heavenly liturgy. Hence, the Eucharist and the church of all ages and all places belong together. The apostle Paul expresses this union of the eucharistic and the ecclesial mystical Body of Christ in language pregnant with meaning: "Because there is one bread, we who are many are one body, for all partake of the one bread" (I Cor 10:17). This is why the Second Vatican Council, quoting the church father Augustine, called the Eucharist "the sign of unity and the bond of love" (SC 47).

Hence, the celebration of the Mass is never just the celebration of one individual community, and still less of one particular group. Even when we attend to the needs of the various groups that exist, we must never lose sight of the totality, but must rather seek in the celebration of the Eucharist to bind together the various groups as the one people of God and as the one family of God.

This is why the way in which the Mass is celebrated is not just a matter for the priest, for the celebrating community, or for a team which prepares the liturgy. The very nature of the Eucharist dictates an obligatory structure for the celebration; the postconciliar liturgical reform has regulated this pattern in such broad terms that there is sufficient room for creativity here, and I believe that we have not yet exhausted all the potential for liturgical creativity. Nevertheless, there are also fixed parts of the service, above all the eucharistic prayers, which are not open to an arbitrary choice by the individual or to a personal creativity in the celebration. The observance of this order of things in the celebration of the Mass has nothing to do with legalism; rather, it is an expression of the worldwide Catholic fellowship which ignores all boundaries and binds us together.

I am glad that so many people have found an increasing joy in the liturgy in recent years. The Second Vatican Council described the liturgical renewal as a sign of the passage of the Holy Spirit through the church (SC 43).

Recognizing Jesus Christ in the Breaking of the Bread

A Meditation on Luke 24:13-35

What does it mean to "recognize" Jesus Christ? Where and how do we recognize him? This question formulates a genuine distress felt by many Christians.

The Experience of the Disciples on the Road to Emmaus

One of the stories in the Bible gives us an answer to this question: the account of the two disciples who, in the aftermath of Good Friday in Jerusalem, are now on their way to the nearby village of Emmaus and encounter Jesus (Luke 24:13-35). They had spent every day in the company of Jesus for nearly three years; they had heard his preaching and experienced his wonderful deeds. But had they really known him? Had they really understood him? It is clear that they had not done so: when things got dangerous, they ran away, and now they were bitterly disappointed and wanted to return to their families.

Along the way, they complained to each other about their suffering and their disappointment. They had hoped that Jesus would fulfill their expectation—and indeed the hope of the people as a whole—by bringing in the kingdom of God for which they were waiting. But things turned out very differently. The high priests succeeded in having Jesus condemned and executed on the cross. By now, it was the third day since all those events had taken place.

When Jesus joined them and asked them why they were so sorrowful, their hearts were so full of bitterness and grief and they were so deeply sunken in their fears and cares that they were completely incapable of recognizing him; "their eyes were kept." Even when Jesus explained to them the meaning of sacred scripture and demonstrated that it was the will of God that he should suffer all these things, their hearts burned, but their eyes remained blind.

It was only at the meal, when Jesus broke the bread with them, that the scales suddenly fell from their eyes and they recognized him. All at once, their sadness was transformed into joy; full, indeed more than full of happiness, they ran back to Jerusalem in order to tell the other disciples of their meeting with Jesus and to say that they had recognized him in the breaking of the bread.

The Experience of Emmaus
in the Testimony of the Church

The experience of the two disciples on the road to Emmaus has been continued and repeated many times at a later date. The Acts of the Apostles tell us that the Christians in the earliest community in Jerusalem came together regularly in order to break bread with one another (Acts 2:46).

We possess many testimonies from the period of the early church which show that participation in the celebration of the Eucharist was a typical activity of Christians.[1] Ignatius, the martyr-bishop of Antioch, wrote that being a Christian meant living in accordance with Sunday.[2] We have the testimonies of non-Christians who said that one could recognize the early Christians by the fact that they assembled on Sundays.[3] During the persecution under Emperor Diocletian, the martyrs of Abitina told their judges: "We cannot renounce our assemblies on Sunday. We cannot live without the Supper of the Lord."[4]

The early Christians in the age of persecution had grasped that the celebration of the Eucharist on Sunday was essential to their identity; it was the source from which they drew life. In the Eucharist, the words

Jesus spoke at the Last Supper become a present reality: he gave his disciples bread and said: "This is my body for you" (1 Cor 11:24; Luke 22:19), and then he said: "This is my blood, which is shed for you" (cf. Mark 14:24; Matt 26:28).

With these words, Jesus meant: this is me, the one who gives himself as a gift for you and for everyone. In these gifts of bread and wine, I am present for you; in them, I give myself to you. Under these appearances, I am in your midst. In these signs of bread and wine, you can recognize me and know who I am and how great is my love for you. For the breaking of the bread and the sharing of the wine express who I am for you—namely, the one who shares with you, who communicates himself to you, who gives himself to you.

In this way, Jesus himself answers the question how we can recognize him and experience him, how we can let ourselves be touched by him. It is the same answer that the disciples received in Emmaus. We can recognize Jesus in the breaking of the bread, that is, in the celebration of the eucharistic meal. In the Eucharist, we can recognize him and know who he is and what he does for us. One of the church fathers said: "That which was visible in Christ has passed over into the sacraments."[5]

The Emmaus Experience Today

The celebration of the Eucharist is the heart and the summit of the life of the Christian and of the church (LG 11). This is why the decline in numbers of those taking part in Sunday Mass is an alarming signal that ought to set our inner alarm bells ringing: it demonstrates that faith is growing less and love is growing cold. We let Jesus' love go unanswered. Are we aware how offensive that is, how ungrateful our behavior is, how much guilt we incur thereby? Some people may say: Well, the times have changed, and we no longer live in the days of the first Christians. That is true, but when it comes to the decisively important issue, is our situation truly so utterly different from theirs?

We too may feel that Jesus is far away, or indeed absent; for us too, it often seems that he is dead. We too, like the two disciples, are often so preoccupied by our own selves, by our problems, plans, and expectations, our daily cares and also our disappointments, that we cannot spare a thought for what really matters in life. Daily living takes up so much of our energy that it is impossible for the weekdays to yield place to Sunday.

In that case, Jesus is no longer present and we have the feeling that we are left to cope with our problems on our own. We shut the lid on so many uncomfortable things and present to the world a seemingly carefree countenance—but how good it would be for us to recognize that we are not alone at all, but that there is one who accompanies us on the road, namely, Jesus. Not only does he listen when we lament and complain; he shares with us. In the breaking of the bread, he shares human suffering and dying with us, while at the same time giving us a share in the new life of the resurrection. He gives himself to us, and with the gift of himself, he gives us (like the two disciples in Emmaus) consolation and hope, joy and bliss.

Consequences of the Emmaus Experience

Naturally, to recognize Jesus in the breaking of the bread also means that it must be possible for others to recognize us Christians in the breaking of the bread—that is, in our sharing and giving. Not for nothing was it said of the first Christians: "They were together and had all things in common" (Acts 2:44). We can share the eucharistic bread only when we also share our daily bread. We read in a description of the way of life of the early Christians: "They love everyone and are persecuted by all. . . . They are poor and make many rich; they lack everything and yet have an abundance of everything."[6]

On the feast of Corpus Christi, we celebrate the eucharistic Lord in public and bear him out onto our streets and city squares. This signifies that the celebration of the Eucharist ought to have an effect on our daily living. We too must be inspired by the same attitude that inspired Jesus when he instituted the Eucharist at the Last Supper in the upper room: "for you," "for all." Just as Jesus makes himself a gift for us, we too should make ourselves a gift for others.

To make ourselves and our life a gift—that is a message that rings strange in the ears of most people today, for one fundamental trait of our society is that we seek to take and to hang onto what we have taken, rather than to give. Many simply cannot get enough, and desperately try to cling to their possessions. This is why there is so little change in our world. Scarcely anything is in movement; indeed, scarcely anything lets itself be moved. This rigid egotism is a sign of death, not of life. For life is born of love, and it is only the one who lays down his life that will find it (Mark 8:35).

We must let ourselves be inspired and motivated by Jesus' breaking of the bread. We must learn anew what it means to share and to give. We need a new culture of generosity, of solidarity, of sharing, and of compassion. This is essential if our society is to continue to be humane at all; and it is just as much a question of our credibility as Christians.

Our watchword must be: let us recognize Jesus Christ in the celebration of Sunday Mass, and let us make ourselves recognizable as Christians by means of the basic attitude that finds expression in the Eucharist. Then we, like the earliest community, will be able to celebrate the breaking of the bread with joy and exultation (Acts 2:46). God's love in Jesus Christ wants to infect us and to become a source of renewal both for our own lives and for the world.

The Presence of Jesus Christ in the Eucharist

A Meditation on John 6

Hunger for Life

The sixth chapter of John's Gospel tells us about people in the wilderness, where nothing grows and no food can be found. It is a place where people die of hunger and thirst, because one cannot survive there for any length of time. With a lack of forethought, they have not taken any food with them—they have only five loaves and two fishes, but what is that for so many? What is that for more than five thousand people? It does not even begin to suffice! Jesus' disciples begin to panic and want to send the people away as quickly as possible into the surrounding villages. But when Jesus tells them to "make the people sit down," the people remain and hold out—and are not disappointed: "They ate their fill."

People at that time were very poor and felt that their leaders had abandoned them. This makes it easy to understand why they believed Jesus was the promised prophet, the messianic king for whom they were hoping, and why they came, seeking to take him by force and make him their "bread-king."

We human beings are driven by needs. We are hungry and need food; we need clothing and somewhere to live; we need work; and (more than ever in today's society) we need an education. All this is the bread of life, in the widest sense of the term, and many millions of people lack all this even today. Jesus was realistic enough to perceive this hunger, and that is why he taught us to pray: "Give us today our daily bread."

But Jesus is aware of another hunger too, the hunger for life to the full. In the synagogue at Capernaum, he says to the people: You seek me because you ate your fill of the bread. You have come in order to get a bread that perishes; but you must seek the food which gives the life that endures, eternal life. Your hunger for the daily bread desires to be satisfied, but there is another hunger and thirst that cannot be satisfied by the daily bread. The daily bread satisfies you for a moment; but there is also a hunger for that which endures, the hunger for eternal life.

These affirmations sound as if they were addressed more to us today than to the people at the time of Jesus. Many people seem wholly absorbed by the hunger for earthly life and by their anxiety to ensure the

satisfaction of their daily needs. They forget, indeed
they suppress, their awareness that life is more and
needs more than eating and drinking, a reasonable standard of prosperity, and the occasional experience of
fun and pleasure. All this may be good for the moment,
but it does not bring happiness nor satisfy our hunger
for true life. Hence, many people today live in a new
and different kind of wilderness. Augustine summa-
rizes the restless early years of life in the famous sen-
tence in his *Confessions*: "Restless is our heart until it
rests in you," that is, in God.[1] Only God is great
enough to satisfy completely all the yearning of our
heart and all our hunger for life.

Salvation in Jesus Christ

People at the time of Jesus—unlike people in our own
society—took the religious dimension for granted, and
they were certainly familiar with the question about
where eternal life was to be found. They begin to be
irritated only when Jesus tells them: "I am the bread of
life." These "I"-statements are characteristic of the
Fourth Gospel, and we find them in many passages: "I
am the light of the world" (John 8:12); "I am the way,
the truth, and the life" (14:8). When he uses these
words, Jesus is saying to them: I am what you seek, I am
what you are asking about—bread, light, truth.

This means that the Christian faith is not a matter of dizzying heights of audacious speculations. The Christian faith is not some kind of higher "gnosis." In the Christian faith, the movement goes in the opposite direction: it is not we who have to ascend into the heavenly heights, but God who descends into the world by becoming a human being and dwelling among us (John 1:14). He is completely one of us, like us in all things but sin (Heb 4:15). He who was in the form of God takes on the form of a slave and is obedient even to death on a cross (Phil 2:6-8).

The Christian faith does not find its orientation in a system of intellectual propositions. Its point of reference is always a concrete person, namely, Jesus Christ. People found this intolerable and irritating: how can this man, whom we know to be the son of Joseph and whose mother we know, make such a claim, presenting himself as the Son of God? The Gospel tells us that they "murmured." Later on, Paul was to write that the message of the cross was a scandal to the Jews and folly to the Gentiles (1 Cor 1:23).

The "murmuring" that began then has never fallen silent, up to the present day; indeed, it has become very loud again today, when many cannot believe in the incarnation of God. They see Jesus as an example of what a good person is, but they look on the incarnation of God as a myth. Others are convinced that God has revealed himself not only in Jesus but also in the many other figures who are venerated in the various religions as bringers of salvation, and they find the claim that salvation is to be found in Jesus alone arrogant and intolerant.

The Gospel replies with tremendous firmness: there is one God, who is the Father of all; there is one Lord, who is the redeemer of all, namely, Jesus Christ, the one mediator between God and human beings (I Tim 2:5); salvation is to be found in no other name (Acts 4:12). He is life, and the bread of life. It is in him, the God-man, that the deepest yearning of the human heart for unending life has found unique fulfillment, so that he himself is the true, abiding, and definitive fulfillment of life.[2] "The one who believes has eternal life." This is why we sing in the *Gloria* of the Mass: "You alone are the Holy One . . . you alone are the Most High." In the hymn for the feast of Corpus Christi, we sing: *Lauda, Sion, salvatorem*: "Praise, O Zion, your Savior, sing in exultation to the one who redeems those who had gone astray!"

The Real Presence of Jesus Christ in the Eucharist

The Gospel goes one step further. Jesus says not only: "I am the bread of life," but also: I give you myself as the bread of life. "The bread which I shall give is my flesh for the life of the world." Those who hear his words are utterly scandalized now: "How can this man give us his flesh to eat?" They find this language totally intolerable. They murmur and take offense, and many abandon Jesus.

This offense has lasted throughout the history of the church, and it continues to be felt today. There have always been attempts to understand as merely symbolic and figurative the words that Jesus spoke at the Last Supper in the upper room: "This is my body"; "This is my blood" (Mark 14:22f. and parallels). But he did not say: "This signifies my body," but rather, "This is my body."

There have been many controversies in the history of theology about this word "is." Naturally, what we have in the Eucharist is not the earthly flesh and blood of Jesus Christ, open to perception by the senses. That was the misunderstanding of the people in Capernaum, and this crudely sensuous interpretation is, in fact, known as the "Capernaist" misunderstanding. On the other hand, we may not react to this position by taking a purely symbolic view.

The church's doctrine responds to both these misunderstandings by maintaining firmly a sacramental understanding. All that one can touch, see, and taste externally by means of the senses is bread and wine; but through faith in Jesus' word we know that, thanks to the working of the Holy Spirit, the true reality which is not accessible to the senses (that which the Middle Ages called the "substance"[3]) is no longer bread and wine, but the body and blood of Christ—and this means, in keeping with the language of the Bible, Jesus Christ himself in the gift that he makes to us of himself. Thus, the forms of bread and wine which the senses can perceive become signs and real symbols of a new reality, that of the risen and exalted Lord; they are filled with this reality and make it present. In this sacramental sense, Jesus' words—"This is my body" and "This is my blood"—are to be understood as designating a reality. And it is in this sacramental sense that we speak of the "real presence," that is, the true, real, and essential presence of Jesus Christ under the signs of bread and wine.[4]

The Catholic Church agrees in this real understanding both with the Orthodox churches and with Lutheran Christians.[5] We can be thankful that we have become aware once again in recent years of the common ground on which we stand. Although some questions remain open, the ecumenical movement has brought us significantly closer to one another.

Many attempts have been made to understand the mystery of the Eucharist more profoundly, but it remains a "mystery of faith." We cannot penetrate it with our understanding, any more than we can fully grasp the mystery of the incarnation; but we can see the inherent connection between these two mysteries. Each provides the basis for the other, and each sheds light on the other.[6] In the Eucharist, the incarnation continues in a new, that is, a sacramental manner, as the martyr-bishop Ignatius of Antioch clearly recognizes. He fights in the same breath against those who call the incarnation a merely outward appearance and those understand the Eucharist as a merely outward appearance: for if one takes such a position, everything is dissolved into mere outward show, and it is only in appearance that we have been saved. Everything is then a mere theater; everything is a huge falsehood.[7]

One of the truly great theologians, Thomas Aquinas, gave us the wonderful Corpus Christi hymn: "I adore you devotedly, hidden Godhead, who are truly hidden under these signs. . . . Eyes, mouth, and hands become unreliable when they meet you: it is only the ear that may be safely believed."[8] This mystery cannot be "solved" by the human understanding; here, the only attitude possible is the attitude of faith: "My heart submits itself totally to you, because when it contemplates you, it loses all its power."[9]

Jesus Christ: Food for Eternal Life

Bread is not meant to be looked at, but to be eaten. The
Eucharist too is given to us so that we may eat it: "Take
and eat," says Jesus at the Last Supper (Matt 26:26),
and he says in the synagogue in Capernaum: "The one
who eats my flesh and drinks my blood has eternal life"
(John 6:54).[10] Just as we receive earthly nourishment
and transform it into our own selves in order that it
may feed and strengthen us, so Jesus Christ enters into
us in communion, in order that he may be in us and we
in him. This is what "communion" means: the most
intimate personal fellowship with Jesus Christ, which
unites us to him in order that we may become one with
him. The church fathers express this in very realistic
language, saying that we become bearers of Christ, and
one body and blood with him, through communion.[11]
They use the image of two candles that melt together
to form one single candle when they speak of what it
means for the communicant to become one with
Christ.[12]

Through this personal union, Jesus truly becomes
our spiritual nourishment. He wishes to feed us and
strengthen us on our path, to heal the sicknesses of our
soul, and to be viaticum (food for the journey) on the
last way we shall take at the end of our lives. Thus the

Eucharist becomes a foretaste of the heavenly wedding feast, and this is why the martyr-bishop Ignatius of Antioch calls it a "medicine of immortality" (*pharmakon athanasias*).[13] Irenaeus of Lyons wrote: "When our bodies share in the Eucharist, they are no longer corruptible, since they have an eternal hope of resurrection."[14]

When we reflect on this profound "mystery of faith," we can understand why the institution of the Eucharist is preceded by the washing of the disciples' feet, as a sign of the purification of the entire person (John 13:4-11). Accordingly, the apostle Paul warns that we must make a distinction between the eucharistic bread and ordinary bread, and that we must examine ourselves: "for whoever eats and drinks unworthily is eating and drinking judgment upon himself" (I Cor 11:29). The church fathers repeat this warning again and again.[15] In the Eastern liturgy, the bishop or the celebrating priest calls out to the faithful before communion: "That which is holy for those who are holy!" The mediaeval theologians spoke of a spiritual communion, meaning that one should not merely receive the sacrament with one's body but in a spiritual attitude of faith. It is unimportant in this context whether one receives on the hand or the tongue; we sin with the tongue at least as often as with the hand. The decisive point is that communion is received reverently, in faith and with a pure conscience.[16]

The fellowship of the eucharistic meal is thus much more than a merely fraternal table fellowship. It is a most intimate fellowship with Jesus Christ and, in him, also with one another. Human fellowship, no matter how important, beautiful, and deep it may be, cannot satisfy our hunger for life, since it encounters its natural boundary when we die. The eucharistic fellowship with the risen Christ crosses over the border of death. It is an anticipation and a foretaste of the fellowship that we shall have in heaven with him and with one another, as the *Magnificat* antiphon on the feast of Corpus Christi says: "O sacred meal in which Christ is our food: memorial of his suffering, fullness of grace, guarantee of the future glory!"

Ecumenism of Life
and Eucharistic Fellowship

Future Perspectives

But now in Christ Jesus you who once were far off
have been brought near in the blood of Christ. For he
is our peace, who has made us both one, and has broken down the dividing wall of hostility . . . so making
peace, that he might reconcile us both to God in one
body through the cross . . . for through him we both
have access in one Spirit to the Father. So then you are
no longer strangers and sojourners, but you are fellow
citizens with the saints and members of the household
of God, built upon the foundation of the apostles and
prophets, Christ Jesus himself being the cornerstone,
in whom the whole structure is joined together and
grows into a holy temple in the Lord; in whom you
also are built into it for a dwelling place of God in the
Spirit. (Eph 2:13-22)

Biblical Foundations

In historical terms, this text speaks of the abolition of
the enmity between Jews and Gentiles. Since this primal

schism between church and synagogue led to all the
later schisms, we can apply this text also to the frag-
mentation of Christianity into various confessional
churches: here too, the Letter to the Ephesians affirms
that the wall of hostility has been broken down and
peace has been established. All of us, Orthodox,
Protestants, members of the Free Churches, and
Catholics, are household members in the one house of
God.

Naturally, we must pay attention to precisely what
the text says. It is not we who have established peace: it
is Jesus Christ who is our peace. It is he who holds the
whole structure together and who bestows growth in
unity with God and with one another. Accordingly,
unity is not the outcome of human endeavor. Growth
in unity is a Pentecostal event.

Foundations of an Ecumenism of Life

In this brief passage, the Letter to the Ephesians
teaches us that ecumenism is based on Jesus Christ—or
to put it more specifically, on the cross and resurrection
of Jesus Christ. In this way, the Letter arms us in
advance against the risk of an ecumenism that might
simply decline into a general humanism which (if taken
to its extreme consequences) would end up in the ide-

ology of freemasonry: "Embrace one another, O ye millions!" The basis of that kind of general humanistic ecumenism is not Jesus Christ, but a colorless universal religion which would claim that we all have one God and need no church, since all the propositions in which the faith is enshrined are completely expendable.

This liberal-rationalistic view is the greatest enemy of the ecumenical movement, since it strips it of the basis and the motivation which gave birth to ecumenism. The foundational statement of the World Council of Churches formulated these basic approaches, and the Second Vatican Council explicitly adopted them when it taught: "Taking part in this movement, which is called ecumenical, are those who invoke the Triune God and confess Jesus as Lord and Savior" (UR 1). These words are an unmistakable affirmation that the ecumenical movement stands on the common ground of the professions of the faith of the as yet undivided church of the first centuries on belief in Jesus Christ as the Son of God and on belief in the triune God. Without these biblical and dogmatic foundations, there is no ecumenism.

When we speak of an ecumenism of life and of a dialogue of life,[1] we are referring to the new life that was bestowed on us when we were baptized in the name of the trinitarian God, that is, life in Jesus Christ and in the Holy Spirit. Through the one Baptism, all the baptized are introduced into the one body of Christ, the one church (Gal 3:28; I Cor 12:13; Eph 4:4). This means that we do not start completely afresh in ecumenical work; our starting point is not that of divided churches which subsequently must come together. In virtue of our common Baptism, there already exists today a fundamental, though imperfect, unity. Reflection on our common Baptism and on the baptismal creed, which we repeat in the Easter Vigil each year, is the point of departure and the point of reference of every ecumenism of life.

Today, when awareness of the foundations of the Christian faith has declined dramatically, such reflection is urgently necessary. Many people—and not only those whose Christianity consists exclusively of the fact that they possess a baptismal certificate—no longer realize what it means to be a Christian and to be baptized, and what it means to be summoned to the new life.

When we lose sight of these foundations, ecumenism risks becoming a wishy-washy affair without any clear contours, something that will sooner or later dissolve into thin air. This is why the Pontifical Council for Unity, after consulting the episcopal conferences of the world, has recommended that they should engage in a dialogue with their partner churches about the mutual recognition of one another's Baptism and about what this Baptism means. In today's ecumenical situation, where we face new difficulties, merely cosmetic repairs are of little use; we must start at the most basic level and ensure that the foundations of the ecumenical movement are stable.

It is only when we clearly perceive these foundations that we will see how scandalous our division is, for it is only then that we will experience the inherent contradiction between the fact that we are *one* body in Jesus Christ yet live in separate churches. We will also realize that we cannot simply accept this situation; nor is it enough to leave the divisions and contradictions untouched and present to the eyes of the world a unity that does not in fact exist. Our divisions deprive us of credibility and are one of the greatest obstacles to world mission. Jesus Christ tore down the walls, but we have constructed new walls and piled up new trenches.

If we take the Letter to the Ephesians seriously, we cannot allow ourselves to imagine that it is a simple matter to leap over these walls and trenches. Nor can we act as if the walls and trenches were nonexistent. It is only in the power of the Spirit of Pentecost that we can overcome them. Where shall we find an ecumenical path that leads forward? The only solution is to cultivate the new life bestowed on us in Baptism, letting it grow and mature. This is called spiritual ecumenism, and is the heart of the ecumenism of life.

An Ecumenical "Intermediary Stage"

We can thank God that we have received so much on this path in recent decades. The wall has indeed already been torn down, but there are still any number of stumbling stones lying around. This is not the fault of "the others" or of "those higher up," people who allegedly refuse to take account of the results of theological study. Such accusations do not lead anywhere useful. Each one of us is a stumbling stone, because there are no Christians who live as they ought.

In ecumenical terms, therefore, we are in what we might call an "intermediary stage." Decisive things have happened. Anyone whose memory goes back over a couple of decades knows that more has occurred in these decades than in the previous centuries. Important texts have been published, bearing witness to a considerable measure of mutual convergence.[2]

Much more important is what has happened in life: Protestant and Catholic Christians no longer look on each other as foes and competitors but see the other as brothers and sisters who live, work, and pray together. We must be grateful for this, and we should not allow the pessimists to speak ill of ecumenism, nor succumb to an apocalyptic pessimism which can see only decadence and decline on every side. At the solemn opening of the Second Vatican Council, Pope John XXIII issued an explicit warning against such prophets of doom.

At the same time, however, we ought not to be ecumenical dreamers who pursue mere utopias. There are two kinds of utopia. The progressive vision no longer sees the pieces of wall which still lie around, nor the trenches—and hence falls flat on its face. This utopia holds that all the differences have been overcome in principle long ago, or that they consist merely of irrelevant disputes among theologians to which one need pay no attention. But can we imagine a Catholic parish priest throwing the tabernacle out of his church because he does not want to have anything different from the Protestants, or a Protestant pastor installing a tabernacle in his church? It is easy to imagine the uproar in both parishes, and the reaction on the part of the faithful would quickly reveal the differences that continue to exist between the two churches.

In addition to the progressive utopia, there is a clericalistic-integralistic utopia, which thinks that the problems can be regulated by formulating as many prohibitions as possible. It is unfortunately the case that some official documents limit themselves to a list of all the things it is forbidden to do, without however indicating any positive paths out of the scandal of division. This is just as unhelpful as the first utopia, for all development—and indeed all life—is suffocated before it has the chance to grow.

Christians are neither utterly gloomy pessimists nor utopians who see everything through rose-colored spectacles. Christians are realists on the basis of their faith, and realists in their lives. All that lives moves from one point to another along a path full of tension; and in this sense, we are in a period of ecumenical transition. We can rejoice that we have reached a number of milestones along the path, but we have not yet attained our goal. This is still a time for growing and maturing, or (as the Letter to the Ephesians says in another passage) a time for building and growing up toward the entire fullness of Christ (4:16).

Ecumenism as a Process of Growth

The biblical images of building and growing play an important role in the debate with those who attack ecumenism from an extreme conservative position—and sadly, such persons are growing in numbers. They admonish us: "No false compromises! There can be no ecumenism at the price of the truth." To this I reply: this is perfectly correct. Love without truth is dishonest, a mere simulacrum of love. The church has been founded once and for all upon the truth of the apostles and prophets (Eph 2:20), and the Holy Spirit maintains her always in the truth. She is the same in all centuries, and we cannot build a new church today. But although she has been set up once and for all, the church is continually built up of living stones (I Pet 2:5); she is the pilgrim people of God en route in the history of the world.

Along this path, the Holy Spirit leads us into the fullness of the truth (John 6:13), helping us grow and mature in the truth which we have recognized. Truth and tradition are not rigidly immobile, something we pass on to other persons as one might pass on a dead coin. Tradition is a living tradition, a process of life; it is "spirit and life" (John 6:63). And we must remind such critics that this is not just something taught by the Second Vatican Council (DV 8); it was already taught by the First Vatican Council in the nineteenth century.[3] It is perfectly in accord with the Catholic tradition to affirm that there exists a progress in knowledge of the truth which was revealed once and for all. One might say that the church "becomes" what she always was and what she always is.

Two great theologians of the nineteenth century elaborated this teaching: Johann Adam Möhler (1796-1838) of Tübingen and the great John Henry Newman (1801-1890). The theological pioneer and master of ecumenical theology, the Dominican Yves Congar

(1904-1995), the centenary of whose birth has just been celebrated, studied the writings of both these scholars and demonstrated long before the Second Vatican Council that there are two paths along which the church grows and transcends her present boundaries to enter into her own future: ecumenism and mission.

In mission, the church's horizon widens as she grows and enters new peoples and cultures; she assimilates their cultures in a critical spirit, penetrating, purifying, and deepening them. This discloses to the church aspects of her own truth that had been hidden up to then. This is what happened in the encounter with the classical hellenistic and Roman culture, and in the encounter with the Germanic and Slavic peoples; this is what is happening today with the African and Asian cultures, and this is what ought to be happening with our modern and postmodern culture, which is subject to such rapid change. Sadly, however, we Christians have grown weary of the battle, and we have largely lost the missionary dynamism and the courage to press forward into new territories. We ask how we might just manage to hold onto as much as possible of what we already possess, rather than finding the courage to make new missionary emphases in our work.

A similar advance is taking place in ecumenism. To some extent, the separated churches and ecclesial communities have preserved and expressed individual aspects of the one truth of the gospel better than we ourselves; this means that we can learn from one another to our mutual enrichment. Let me mention only one example. In recent decades, we have learned much from our Protestant fellow Christians about the significance of the Word of God, the reading and the exposition of sacred scripture; at the present day, they are learning from us about the significance of liturgical symbols and liturgical celebrations.

Ecumenism is not a question of selling off everything at knock-down prices, nor is it a process of impoverishment in which one abandons one's own identity and frivolously throws overboard things that were sacred to earlier generations. Ecumenism is a process whereby life itself grows. The pope has called ecumenism an "exchange of gifts and presents."[4] At one and the same time, we give and receive in plenty. As the First Letter of Peter puts it, we are to serve one another, each with the gift of grace that particular person has received (4:10). Or, as the Church Assembly in Berlin put it: we are to be a blessing for each other.

Many intermediate steps are necessary on this path of growth and maturity. One who refuses to take these small steps deprives himself of the possibility of making great progress one day in the future: one who wants to have everything all at once and to have the final result now will end up achieving nothing. All life unfolds according to the law of steps, and in keeping with the laws of growth. I once read on a calendar page the following words: "Patience is tamed passion." Another page of the same calendar declared: "Patience means courage, endurance, strength." For, as Charles Péguy said, patience is "the little sister of hope."

Practical Possibilities of an Ecumenism of Life

These quotations are not given here by way of a cheap consolation. Rather, my intention in the present section is to indicate some concrete ways in which an ecumenism of life may be put into practice. A more detailed list may be found in the Ecumenical Directory of the Pontifical Council for Unity, the Ecumenical Charter of the European episcopal conferences, or corresponding publications of the individual dioceses. Here, I look at the three basic functions of the church: bearing witness to the faith, celebrating the liturgy, and the diaconal service of human beings.

Let us begin with testimony to the faith. This is not in the least restricted to the clergy. Every Christian is commissioned in his or her own way to bear witness to the faith, and testimony to the faith in daily living is fundamental. Particular importance attaches to reading and reflecting on sacred scripture in common. The Bible led to our separation, and it is by means of the Bible that we must once again become one. There are many possibilities of sharing biblical work, such as ecumenical Bible study groups. There is by now a well-established custom that Protestant and Catholic clergy both preach at ecumenical liturgies of the Word. We can also add collaboration in religious education in school and in adult education. It is important here that we first study the theological results of ecumenical dialogue, so that we can analyze what practical consequences they might have for us.

Let us now turn to the liturgy, a term that embraces more than the celebration of the Eucharist or of the Lord's Supper. There can be no doubt that, above all for us Catholics, the Eucharist is the center and summit; but things have developed in the wrong direction, if we concentrate *all* our attention on it, since the Eucharist can be a high point only if it is surrounded by other acts of worship. Our first step must therefore be to make full use of ecumenical forms of the liturgy of the Word, Vespers, prayers for peace, memorial services, youth worship, services inspired by Taizé, worship with small groups early in the morning or late at night, celebrations in Advent, agape celebrations, services which recall the worshipers' Baptism, ecumenical pilgrimages, and so forth. There are liturgical calendars for ecumenical services on the various feasts and other occasions in the course of the church's year.

Finally, we have the field of diaconal service. Here, there has been a considerable ecumenical development, but we could do still more together. Perhaps the fact that money is getting scarcer everywhere may indeed compel us to unite our forces. I mention only a few examples: ecumenical social-work stations, hospice work, work among the elderly, visiting the sick, pastoral care in hospitals, telephone lines for people in need, pastoral care in reconvalescent centers, missions in railway stations, work with the mass media. One could extend this list, of course; and we must add the many various forms of encounters, for example, meetings of Catholic and Protestant pastors and deans, joint meetings of parish and deanery councils, groups where the clergy meet for prayer, neighborhood discussion groups. All of these help one to see the situation beyond one's own backyard, so to speak. Last but not least, we have the working groups composed of members from the various churches on the level of individual cities, deaneries, and countries.

The reader will see that even today, much more is possible than most people realize. If we were to put into practice what is possible today, we would make significant progress on our journey!

The Question of Eucharistic Fellowship

There remains the question of fellowship in the Eucharist or in the Lord's Supper. For us, the Eucharist is the sacrament of faith; each time we celebrate it, we hear the words "Let us proclaim the mystery of faith" after the words of institution and consecration. This is why the assembled community responds at the end of the canon of the Mass with "Amen—yes, we believe!" and why this "Amen" is repeated by each individual who receives communion: "Amen—yes, this *is* the body of Christ!" Naturally, this "Amen" signifies more than a merely intellectual assent to a dogma. It entails a yes that must be uttered by one's whole life and must be made credible by a Christian way of living. And this is why we cannot accept a universal, open invitation to communion—not even for those Catholics who are present at the Mass.

The basic precondition for admission to the Eucharist is the question whether one can say "Amen" to all that the Catholic faith believes takes place in the celebration of the Mass. One must be able to say this "Amen" with an honest heart and in union with all the assembled community, both at the end of the eucharistic prayer and when one receives communion; and one must bear witness with one's life to this "Amen." Luther and Calvin could not have spoken such an "Amen"; nor would they have wanted to do so, since their protest was directed, not only against the papacy, but most vehemently of all against the Mass. We may thank God that we have come much further now in our discussions of this question with the Lutherans; but even today, serious differences remain.

This is why we may formulate, as a rule of thumb, that one goes to communion in the church to which one belongs. There are good biblical reasons for this rule (1 Cor 10:17) and a long-shared tradition that lasted into the 1970s.

But there is another basic rule too: the council says that the "desire for grace" recommends worship in common in certain cases (UR 8). Similarly, Catholic canon law says: "The salvation of souls is the highest law" (canon 1752). This is why Catholic Church law envisages that in specific, extraordinary circumstances, a non-Catholic Christian may be admitted to communion, provided he shares our eucharistic faith and bears witness to it in his life.[5] It is, of course, impossible for canon law to offer a list of every conceivable individual instance; it indicates a binding framework within which one may act responsibly in pastoral situations.

In his 1995 encyclical on ecumenism, the pope offered a more spiritual description of the meaning of the prescriptions of canon law: "It is a source of joy to note that Catholic ministers are able, in certain particular cases, to administer the sacraments of the Eucharist, Penance, and Anointing of the Sick to Christians who are not in full communion with the Catholic Church but who greatly desire to receive these sacraments, freely request them, and manifest the faith which the Catholic Church professes with regard to these sacraments."[6] It is clear that this affirmation was very important in the pope's eyes, for he repeated it literally eight years later in his encyclical on the Eucharist.[7]

I am confident that our priests have sufficient pastoral and spiritual sensitivity to find solutions, in agreement with their bishop and following the guidelines laid down by the pope, that will do justice to the individual personal situations and to the great variety of life itself.

Spiritual Ecumenism as the Heart of the Ecumenical Movement

Up to this point, we have spoken of the official ecclesiastical possibilities open to the ecumenism of life, but this is only one side of the coin. The church is not only an institution; she also has a charismatic dimension, and we must now speak of this. We have already noted that it is the task of the Holy Spirit to lead us more deeply into the truth and the reality of salvation in the intermediary time between the "already" and the "not yet" (John 14:26; 15:26; 16:13). This takes place through the multiplicity of charisms (Rom 12:4-8; I Cor 12:4-11).

The Letter to the Ephesians speaks of the foundations of the apostles and of the prophets (2:20), referring not to the prophets of the Old Testament, but to New Testament prophets, that is, prophetically gifted men and women who draw on the creativity of the Holy Spirit to find new words for the Good News and bring it "up to date." Where the church has become tired and has adapted herself too much to the world, these persons formulate the driving force of the gospel with prophetic criticism. They discover in a constructive manner new Christian and ecumenical forms of living, radical in the positive sense of this word; through practicing these modes of life they meet the challenges that face the church by opening up the path into the future.

In past centuries, these prophets were often founders of religious orders, who lived and taught a new spirituality not only for their own order but for many laypersons too: Benedict, Francis of Assisi, Ignatius Loyola, Teresa of Avila, Thérèse of Lisieux, and many others. In the period in which they lived, which was often a period of decline, they introduced a new upsurge of life in the church, giving her a spiritual vitality which has lasted across the centuries to the present day.

Today, the Spirit of God has inspired a great variety of spiritual movements, with communities of laypersons or families, groups devoted to evangelization, and charismatic communities. Similar things are happening in many Catholic religious orders and in monasteries of brothers and sisters and communities in the Protestant churches. Much still remains to be done in this field in Germany, and this is why I was happy to note that Christians, most of them young people, from a total of 170 different movements assembled in Stuttgart early in May, 2004. They did not compete with one another but made a positive impression on the public whom they addressed, urging that Europe should organize its life on Christian principles. I hope that the World Youth Day in 2005 will provide further powerful inspiration.

Pope John Paul II is surely right to say that these movements and communities are a response by the Holy Spirit to the "signs of the times." Many of them are involved in ecumenical work, developing new forms of ecumenical living in common that point the way ahead for the church, and they have formed ecumenical networks. The founding father of the spiritual ecumenical movement, the French priest Paul Couturier (d. 1953), spoke of an invisible monastery in which fervent prayer would be raised for the coming of the Spirit of unity.

The heart of ecumenism is not papers and documents for theological study. No doubt these do have their importance, but one sometimes cannot resist the impression that there is far too much printed paper circulating in today's church. At Pentecost, the Holy Spirit did not appear in the form of paper but in the form of tongues of fire—and, fortunately, fire burns up useless paper! The essential requirement is spiritual ecumenism. Ecumenism began, before the council, in groups of friends; today, it will receive a fresh impetus above all in groups of friends, communities, and places where people share their lives with one another.

The Second Vatican Council calls spiritual ecumenism the soul of the ecumenical movement (UR 8). The council lists the following elements: personal conversion; sanctification of one's life; mutual forgiveness instead of continually reproaching the other side for its past errors; purification of the memory in view of the mistakes committed by one's own side; humble service and selfless love (UR 6-9).

Prayer for unity is of decisive importance, since we cannot "produce" unity—ultimately, it is a gift of the

Holy Spirit, and we can only pray for the Spirit: *Veni, sancte Spiritus!* "Come, Holy Spirit!" We can do nothing better than imitate what the disciples, the holy women, and the mother of the Lord did after Jesus had ascended into heaven: they gathered in the upper room in which he had celebrated the Last Supper and persevered in unanimous prayer for the coming of the Spirit (Acts 1:14). The "Week of Prayer for Christian Unity" in January ought therefore to be the focal point of all our ecumenical endeavors in the course of the church's year.

In addition to prayer and personal sanctification, the council speaks of the reform and renewal of the church. The council affirms that the church is "always in need of purification" and must "follow constantly the path of penance and renewal" (LG 8). This is a new language: the church no longer speaks of converting others but insists that conversion begins with our own selves. However, although a purely institutional reform and the introduction of structures of *communio* are highly desirable, they do not begin to suffice. If they are not imbued with a new spirituality of community, all they lead to are purified, but soulless, organizations.

A spirituality of community means recognizing in the other person my brother and sister in the faith, sharing their joys and their sufferings, perceiving their wishes, and helping them in their needs. A spirituality of community entails the ability to see above all the positive element in the other person, so that one can receive it as a divine gift for oneself too. Finally, a spirituality of communion means "making way" for the brother and sister, so that "each one bears the other's burden" (Gal 6:2), resisting the temptations to rivalry, distrust, and petty jealousies.[8]

Those who are familiar with the situation in the churches and in the individual parishes and with the relationships between the churches know that much remains to be done here; but they also know that even today a great deal is, in fact, being done in many communities—more than most people realize. Much preparatory work is being done on the ground level to make a renewed ecumenical impetus for the churches a real possibility. I place a very high value on this spiritual ecumenism in so many spiritual communities.

What Is the Goal of Our Journey?

What is the ultimate goal of all this? What is the ecumenical goal? Various answers are given to this question, but this is not surprising, since differing ideas of the essential nature of the church necessarily lead to differing ideas of the unity of the church.

The goal envisaged by Protestants, especially on the

continent of Europe, is content with a basic consensus in the interpretation of the gospel, but broadly speaking leaves the institutional form of the church open. This means that each confession is more or less free to retain its present ordering—with presbyters, synods, or a mixed form. As Protestant theology understands it, the kind of institutional unity that exists among Catholics, above all in the Petrine ministry of the pope, is not necessary; indeed, for many it is not even desirable, and for some it is wholly unacceptable.

Catholics envisage a different goal, inspired by the account in the Acts of the Apostles of the earliest community in Jerusalem: "They devoted themselves to the apostles' teaching and fellowship, to the breaking of bread and the prayers" (2:42). Accordingly, the Catholic position insists on visible unity: unity in faith, in the sacraments, and in the apostolic ordained ministry (cf. UR 2). Far from being a handicap, this unity, which finds its most visible expression in the Petrine ministry, is in fact our strength. Pluralism is both possible and desirable when we are working out what this visible unity means in practice; pluralism is not a defect, but rather shows how rich the unity is. In this sense, Catholics too wish to see not a church of monolithic uniformity but a unity where variety flourishes.

One cannot draw up in advance a blueprint for how such a varied ecumenical unity ought to look at some future date; no architect today can sketch the future ecumenical form of the church. In an ecumenism of life, it must suffice to keep the basic goal before our eyes and to do what is possible here and now. The path of ecumenism is not lit up from start to finish like an airport runway. It is more like the path taken by a wanderer guided by his lantern, which provides light as we actually move forward.

Ecumenism in a Worldwide Perspective

One final aspect of the ecumenism of life is very important to me. The ecumenism of life means that we widen our horizons and think in a worldwide perspective which is truly Catholic.

In the last few years, I have had the opportunity to look at the situation of the church in Germany from the outside, not only from Rome (which some would perhaps consider a disadvantage) but from a worldwide perspective, on my many journeys around the world. While this has certainly led me to appreciate anew the advantages of the "German system," I also note the extent to which we in Germany are obsessed by our own problems. This leads—not only within the church, but clearly also in general societal terms—to an inability to put reforms into practice and to an immobility which suffocates all life. The German church is urgently in need of fresh air from outside. We still have to discover the church in Europe: do we know the other European churches? Voyages of exploration in other European countries need not limit themselves to normal tourist holidays but could certainly enrich our ecumenism too.

I have often said that ecumenism must be extended eastward: with the extension of the European Union to include former communist states, this kind of ecumenism has indeed become a matter of urgency. The integration of the Eastern European countries into the European Union is the greatest challenge of the new century, offering unique possibilities to us; but it can succeed only if we also welcome into our family the Orthodox churches which have so profoundly influenced the culture and mentality of these peoples for many centuries. This is particularly true of the Russian Orthodox Church. Even a superficial acquaintance with the icons, the liturgical hymns, and the ancient churches of Eastern Europe is enough to show what a rich religious culture exists there, with the potential to teach a great deal to us in the West, who have become so poor in religious terms. Ecumenism with Eastern Europe is a vital question, if Europe as a whole is to survive.

In addition to the eastward expansion, I should like to speak also of an ecumenical expansion to the south. By now, we have good relationships with the traditional churches (especially the Anglicans and Lutherans) in Africa, Asia, and Latin America; but we are confronted there with a tremendous growth in Pentecostal churches and Evangelical groups. With some of them, we can build up fruitful relationships, but others are so aggressively fundamentalistic and proselytizing that it is exceedingly difficult (though not altogether impossible) to engage in a dialogue with them.

Many old and new sects and neoreligious movements (New Age, Scientology, so-called youth sects, and so forth) flourish in our own societies. A profound change is taking place throughout the world at present, both in ecumenical work and in the religious landscape as a whole. New ecumenical challenges face us—to say nothing of the encounter with Islam.

Europe has a rich cultural inheritance, marked deeply by the spirit of Christianity. There is no Europe without Christianity. But it is Europe's tragedy that one of the causes of modern secularism was the division of the European churches: sects and neoreligious movements are now moving rapidly into the empty space created by secularism. We can face up to this challenge only with united forces—and that means: only in the spirit of ecumenism.

Hope That Is Not Put to Shame

I should like to conclude this essay with a prayer by Father Couturier, which tells us what we may hope for and how we should pray for it:

> Lord Jesus Christ,
>> you prayed that all might be one.
> We pray for the unity of Christians,
>> as you will it
>> and in the manner in which you will it.
> May your Spirit permit us
>> to suffer the pain of division,
>> to recognize our guilt,
>> and to hope beyond all hope.

"To hope beyond all hope"—that is possible for Christians, and this means that we may not join the know-it-alls who are ever ready to present their objections. Let us keep the torch of our hope burning! This hope should blaze out on Christian faces, for as Christians we have every reason to hope. We can safely put our trust in the Spirit of God, who inspired the ecumenical movement; and he is a God of surprises. He will finish what he has begun—when, and as, he himself wills. The Spirit will show the world that Jesus Christ is our peace. He is the peace of the world.

Sacrament of Unity—
Plurality of Aspects

*Fundamental Theological Reflections
on the Eucharist*

The Eucharist as the Testament of Jesus

"On the night before he suffered," "on the night when he was betrayed": when the church specifies this dating during the celebration of the Eucharist, she explains the historical and substantial reason for what she is doing. She traces the Eucharist back to its institution by Jesus on the evening before his death and sees his will to institute the sacrament not only as the unique point in history at which the celebration began but also as the abiding substantial norm for her celebration of the Mass.

The historical-critical examination of the four New Testament accounts of the Last Supper has often called into question this historical and substantial legitimation of the Eucharist, thereby positing a gulf between

84

Jesus and the church, and between the Last Supper and the Eucharist.[1] In this case, scholars in the past and the present see Jesus in the tradition of the prophetical critique of the temple cult and understand the "breaking of the bread" in the early church as a meal held in common, with no cultic significance nor any special connection with the last meal of Jesus; such scholars argue that it was only in hellenistic Christian groups that these meals were reshaped into a sacramental Lord's Supper on the pattern of pagan cultic mysteries.[2] This interpretative approach, however, does not take us beyond very general analogies, since we cannot explain on the basis of the cultic mysteries the double gesture that is characteristic of the narratives of the Last Supper, namely, the breaking and sharing of the bread, and the drinking from one common cup. These gestures are completely at home in the rite of solemn meals (or of the Passover meal itself) in Judaism.[3] This is true above all of that element which gave the entire ritual at a very early date the name "Eucharist": this is derived from the praise of God (*beraka; eulogia, eucharistia*) that the father as head of the household uttered before the meal over the third cup with wine, the "cup of blessing" (cf. I Cor 10:16).[4]

When we look more closely at the narratives, we see that Jesus did not simply take over already-existing Jewish eating customs at his last meal: he also altered these customs and gave them a new accent, in two ways. First, diverging from the Jewish practice, Jesus gave all those sitting at table the cup of the head of the house, inviting them to drink from it; and second, he accompanied the breaking and sharing of the bread with interpretative words.[5] This means that ultimately there is no analogy to the last meal of Jesus that cannot be contained within any of the customary categories.[6]

The fact that the four New Testament accounts of the Last Supper present different versions indicates, however, that we cannot simply assume that they give us the *ipsissima verba* of the Lord. Rather, his words and his action come to us through the medium of the faith and the liturgy of the early church. Paul explicitly designates his account of the Last Supper as a tradition which he has received "from the Lord" (I Cor 11:23).[7] Since older elements of the tradition are handed on in a variety of forms in all the texts, it is scarcely possible to reconstruct the earliest form of the tradition, still less to identify exactly the original words with which Jesus instituted the Eucharist and interpreted it; at most, one might propose a hypothetical answer to these questions.[8] This does not compromise the historical credibility of the Last Supper narratives, since these concur in relating the unique event, devoid of all analogies, which—even from a purely historical perspective—can be explained adequately only by recourse to the person of Jesus himself.

This is all the more true when we bear in mind that the words and gestures of Jesus that these narratives transmit are completely in keeping with his message and his behavior: their inherent logic can be understood only against the background of the life of Jesus.[9] It is characteristic of Jesus' proclamation that he not only announces the imminent coming of the *basileia* (royal sovereignty) of God but also links this to his own coming, that is, to his own person; and it is characteristic that he uses the image of a meal to portray the coming of the *basileia* and anticipates this coming in celebratory meals. His words at the Last Supper look ahead to the *eschaton*, showing that his last meal too is governed by the perspective and dynamism of the irrupting *basileia* (Mark 14:25). This logion also shows that Jesus remained faithful to this message that he had proclaimed, even in face of his rejection and of his impending death. God's faithfulness is manifested even—or precisely—where human beings are unfaithful, and it is now more than ever that God binds his salvation to the person of Jesus and appoints him to be the "servant of the Lord" who lays down his life in vicarious atonement "for the many" (Mark 14:24; I Cor 11:24, alluding to Isa 53:10ff.). Hence, by means of his vicarious death for the many, he institutes the new covenant in his blood (Luke 22:20; I Cor 11:25, alluding to Jer 31:31).[10] At the Last Supper, Jesus proclaims this new salvific reality and, at the same time, presents symbolically the new community of salvation under the signs of the bread and wine which he distributes. Finally, he identifies himself explicitly with the gifts of bread and wine in this meal and thus makes it clear that he himself, in the gift he makes of his own person, is the new covenant, the eschatological reality of salvation.

Accordingly, Jesus' words and gestures at his last meal are the synthesis of his entire life and at the same time the anticipatory interpretation of his dying. They are guaranteed (so to speak) by his life and above all by his dying; without his life and his dying, they would be merely an uncovered check.[11] When they are seen in connection with his life and his dying, they are the testament of Jesus, through which he wishes to remain present with and for those who belong to him. The self-bequest of Jesus, in order that he may be an abiding presence with us, is the point of departure and the basis of the Eucharist.[12]

There is complete agreement between the Catholic doctrine of the Eucharist and the Protestant doctrine of the Lord's Supper, as far as this point of departure in the testament of Jesus is concerned. This testament provided the key to Luther throughout his interpretation of the Lord's Supper, which he understood as a synthesis of the incarnation and death of Christ. By expounding the *testamentum* one-sidedly as the assurance of the promise of the forgiveness of sins, however, he necessarily emphasized the aspect of the passive reception of the sacrament in faith, playing off this aspect against that of giving and of giving one's own self. Accordingly, Luther makes a sharp distinction between the *sacramentum*, which is received passively, and the *sacrificium*, which is performed actively—and which he rejects very vigorously. His doctrine of the Lord's Supper has a wholly katabatic basis in a Christology "from above"; he discards altogether the anabatic element of the movement "upward" from "below."[13]

If, however, we consider the bequest Jesus makes of himself, it is not difficult to discern two dimensions. In the words spoken at the Last Supper, Jesus interprets the laying down of his life by means of passive verbs: he speaks of the body that is given up, the blood that is poured out. These semitic formulations cast a reverent veil over the fact that it is God himself who is acting here—and that Jesus' obedience is his response to this divine action. Since he owes to God the Father all that he is, he gives thanks and praise when he makes the new reality of salvation proleptically present at the Last Supper. This thanksgiving is the verbal expression of that sacrifice which is his own personal gift of self to the Father's will. Hence there is nothing arbitrary about the sacrificial language of the shedding of his blood that we find in Matthew's version (26:28, alluding to Exod 24:8): it is appropriate and therefore necessary.[14] The gift of himself "for the many," in which Jesus lets himself be consumed, corresponds to his sacrificial gift of self to the Father. Thus it is precisely in his gift of self to the Father in the Last Supper that Jesus makes himself the gift of salvation for human beings.

Jesus' final meal thus reveals not only his mission but also his deepest being: existence from God and for God, and hence at the same time existence for human beings. He is *eucharistia* and *eulogia*, thanksgiving and blessing, in his own person. In this comprehensive sense, the person of Jesus is the point on which everything turns, and Christology provides the background to the Eucharist and the correct approach to understanding it. And this means, with reference to the discussion by contemporary scholars, that every purely functional or purely existential approach to the understanding of the Eucharist is inadequate *a priori*.[15]

The Eucharist as Memorial (Anamnesis)

If we understand the foundations of the Eucharist in the radically christological manner that I have proposed here, we cannot see the Mass as something added onto the Christ-event (and especially to the event of his cross), still less as a supplement to this; nor may we understand it as the continuation or repetition of the crucifixion. Rather, the Eucharist is governed by the law of historical uniqueness ("once and for all," as the Letter to the Hebrews says) which applies to the event of Christ and of his cross, so that its relationship to this event can be described only by means of the biblical category of *memoriale* (*zikkaron; anamnēsis; memoria*), the "remembrance" which makes a past reality present.

The accounts of the Last Supper in Paul and Luke already have the formula: "Do this in memory of me" (Luke 22:19; I Cor 11:24f.). Scholars do not agree on the origin of this command to repeat what Jesus has done.[16] The attempt to derive it from the hellenistic meal in memory of the dead has rightly been abandoned today, and it has been shown that there are serious historical problems with the attempt of the theology of "mysteries" to derive it from the mystery religions; today, interest concentrates on identifying a provenance from the Old Testament and from Judaism.[17] At any rate, the biblical understanding of memorial refers not to a subjective act of remembering but to a liturgical-sacramental celebration of remembrance in which the salvific deed, which belongs to the past, is made objectively present by means of real sym-

bols. This is true, for example, of the feast of Taber-
nacles (Lev 23:33ff.) and above all of the celebration
of the Passover feast as the day when Israel remembered
its liberation from the slavery of Egypt (Exod 12:14).
Thus, each person in every generation is obliged "to see
himself as if he had gone forth out of Egypt."[18] The
salvific deed, which belongs to the past, is rendered
present by means of the liturgy so that it may be placed
before God: appeal is made to what God has done in
the past so that he too may remember it and bring his
own deed to its eschatological fulfillment. The remembrance which looks back to the past, in order that the
past event may be actualized in the present, is thus
linked to an eschatological look ahead to the future fulfillment: all three temporal dimensions are brought
together in a synthesis by the biblical "memorial."

At a very early date, the church fathers attempted to
draw on the typological thinking found in scripture in
order to elaborate the idea of the objective "making-
present" of the work of salvation in the sacraments.
Later, they drew on the Platonic idea of a real symbol
in order to help explain the Eucharist.[19] For Thomas
Aquinas, the Eucharist, like every sacrament, is a *signum
rememorativum* of the work of salvation which took place
once and for all, a *signum demonstrativum* of the salvation
which takes place in the present, and a *signum prognos-
ticum,* anticipating the eschatological banquet in the

kingdom of God.[20] The well-known *Magnificat* antiphon
on the feast of Corpus Christi employs poetic language
to express this threefold dimension: *recolitur memoria passionis eius, mens impletur gratia et futurae gloriae nobis pignus
datur.*[21] In this comprehensive sense, the eucharistic
liturgy too speaks, immediately after the institution
narrative, of the memorial of Jesus Christ: of his death,
his resurrection, his ascension, and his return.

Sadly, this grandiose unified vision was lost to sight
in the course of the Middle Ages. In the aftermath of
the second eucharistic controversy in the eleventh century, archetype and image, type, symbol, and *figura* on
the one hand parted company with *veritas* on the other.
Originally, a "symbol" meant something that in a certain sense is what it signifies; now, a "symbol" was
understood as something that is not genuinely what it
signifies.[22] In order to ward off the danger of a pure
"symbolic understanding" and to hang onto the doctrine of the reality of Jesus' presence in the Eucharist,
the real presence of his flesh and blood was separated
from the anamnetic-symbolic making-present of the
sacrifice of the cross; in this way, it remained possible
to explain the presence of the person who brought salvation and of the fruit of his salvation, but it was no
longer possible to explain the presence of the event of
salvation itself. The sacrament and the sacrifice of the
Eucharist had to be detached from one another: since it

was no longer possible to understand the Eucharist as a sacramental real symbol of the passion of Christ, the sacrificial character of the Eucharist and its relationship to the sacrifice of the cross presented an utterly insoluble problem.[23] It is only against this background that we can fully understand the debates about the sacrifice of the Mass in the Reformation period. Basically, neither side in the sixteenth century possessed categories adequate to the solution of this question. The Council of Trent did indeed succeed in achieving a satisfactory conceptual formulation with the help of the categories of *repraesentatio, memoria,* and *applicatio,*[24] so that it could rebut the Protestant accusation that Catholics viewed the Mass in an idolatrous manner, as an independent sacrifice supplementary to the sacrifice of the cross. But the many theories about the sacrificial character of the Mass in the post-Tridentine period show how little this dogmatic clarification had actually succeeded in furnishing an adequate theological clarification of the *repraesentatio passionis.*

It was only the biblical-liturgical and pastoral renewal in the twentieth century that created a new situation and thereby opened up new possibilities for ecumenical dialogue.[25] Within Catholic theology, the fundamental theological concern of Odo Casel's "theology of the mysteries" (which must be distinguished from the historical arguments put forward in support of it, and from individual points of his theological explanation), concerning the real-symbolic making-present of the work of salvation which had occurred once and for all, found a considerable measure of acceptance, and was finally accorded official recognition by the Second Vatican Council.[26]

The renewal of the theology of the Word of God proved even more important, and more helpful in the ecumenical context, for the understanding of the objective presence of the sacrifice of the cross which had happened once and for all in the past. For Paul, the celebration of the Lord's Supper is the proclamation of the death of the Lord "until he comes" (I Cor 11:26). This means that the celebration of the Eucharist is an embodied word, the public and solemn proclamation of the unique historical event which becomes a presence, or opens up its presence, by means of this utterance and thus takes on public validity, a word of consolation and of challenge both for the individual and for the community.[27] Hence, just as the Jewish prayers at meals were anamneses of God's salvific deeds, so the Eucharist is a memorial in words and actions of the death and resurrection of Jesus which makes these events present, together with the prayer for his coming: *Maranatha!* (I Cor 16:22).

We may sum up by saying that the institution by Jesus is the point of departure and the basis of the

Eucharist, and that the anamnesis of Christ forms the
inner unity of the various aspects of the Eucharist.
Here, the death and resurrection of Jesus Christ are
made present sacramentally; here, the Lord who is present under the forms of bread and wine is praised; the
community prays urgently for his definitive coming.
Thus, the Eucharist mediates fellowship (*communio*)
with the Lord. The presence of the person and work of
Jesus Christ, mediated sacramentally by the memorial
in words and actions, is the inner basis which unites the
various aspects of the Eucharist.[28]

The Eucharist as Thanksgiving and Sacrifice

Both the institution by Jesus and the anamnesis of his
salvific work took place, and take place, in the course
of thanksgiving. The basic attitude of the human person before God, to whom we owe everything, is thanksgiving. In the history of salvation, giving thanks is the
clearest expression of the fact that our position is
purely that of persons who receive the deeds and the
gifts of salvation. This is why praise and thanksgiving
(*beraka*) are not simply one particular component but
are the basic element of the Jewish prayers at meals and
above all of the Passover liturgy. *Eulogia* and *eucharistia*
are constitutive elements of Jesus' institution of his

Supper too (Mark 14:22f. and parallels; I Cor 11:24).[29] Thus the noun *eucharistia* became at a very early date the term for the entire celebration of the Supper of the Lord.[30] From the very earliest times until the present day, the celebration of the Eucharist in the narrower sense of the term has begun with the invitation *Gratias agamus,* "Let us give thanks to the Lord, our God!" This is followed by a prayer of thanksgiving which proclaims and comments on God's deeds of salvation.[31] The Lord's Supper is a celebration of remembrance which gives praise to God: this has rightly been seen as the basic form of the Mass.[32]

The idea of giving thanks was linked at an early date to the idea of sacrifice. The Old Testament is familiar with the sacrifice of praise (*toda*), in which bread and wine played an important role,[33] and with the concept of *hostia laudis* (Ps 50:14, 23; cf. Pss 116:17; 119:108). This concept is taken up by the Letter to the Hebrews (13:15), whence it also found its way into the Roman canon. In this way, scripture personalizes the idea of sacrifice (cf. Ps 40:7; 51:18f.; Heb 10:5-10); most importantly of all, the vicarious gift which the Servant of Yahweh makes of his life is understood not in terms of the technical sacrificial cult but in terms of martyrdom, that is, as the total gift of his person.[34] Drawing on Philo's spiritualization of the Old Testament ideas about sacrifice, the church fathers were able at a very

early date to understand the Eucharist as a sacrifice.[35]
In Irenaeus of Lyons, the gifts of bread and wine stand
in the foreground as a response to the gnostic con-
tempt for material things; they are, as it were, a real-
symbolic expression of the sacrificial mentality which
expresses itself personally in giving thanks. Hence,
there is no great gulf separating *gratias agamus* from
offerre, from *oblatio* (*prosphora, anaphora*), or indeed from
sacrificium (*thysia*). This means that when greater promi-
nence is gradually attached to the element of *oblatio*
within the concept of *eucharistia*, this merely makes more
explicit something that in fact existed from the outset.[36]

There is no reason to object to such a process, which
can be very fruitful, provided that it preserves the pro-
portions of the totality and does not isolate one single
element. In the course of the Middle Ages, however,
this unity of the totality was lost to view.[37] The offering of the gifts of bread and wine with the prayer of
thanksgiving was no longer seen as the sacramental
form in which the one sacrifice of Jesus Christ was
remembered and became present, and this entailed the
risk that the sacrifice of the Mass might be viewed as
an autonomous sacrificial rite. It was against this that
the Reformers protested. They could no longer understand the Eucharist as the effective sacramental making-

present of the sacrifice of the cross, but only as a sacrifice of thanksgiving for the forgiveness of sins which they had received.[38] The debate about this controversial question is exceedingly difficult, but a consensus is slowly being achieved today. This presupposes a rediscovery of the sacramental meaning of the Eucharist: we must learn to understand the Eucharist as a sacramental form, the substance of which is the one sacrifice of Jesus Christ.[39]

This, of course, is only one aspect of the problem—and the easier aspect. The other aspect, which is much more difficult in the ecumenical context, is the extent to which the Eucharist not only makes present the sacrifice of Jesus Christ but is also a sacrifice offered by the church; or, to put it more precisely, whether and to what extent the action in which the church gives thanks and offers sacrifice is the sacramental form of the presence of Christ's sacrifice. This question poses in an acute manner the basic problem whether and to what extent the Eucharist possesses not only a katabatic ("descending") but also an anabatic ("ascending") dimension whereby the church, as the body of Christ, is drawn into his one sacrifice and, as the bride of Christ, shares in obedient submission in offering his sacrifice.[40] For scripture, this is not fundamentally inconceivable, as we see in all those many instances—for example, in the Psalms—where the human answer to the Word of God is itself in turn understood as the Word of God. Giving and receiving are not antithetical actions here: rather, each entails the other.

Since thanksgiving is the basic form of the Eucharist, it follows that the primary meaning of the eucharistic celebration is the *cultus divinus*, the glorification, veneration, praise, and acclamation of God which is performed by recalling his mighty deeds. In our society, which is orientated to the satisfaction of human needs, it is becoming increasingly difficult to appreciate this cultic aspect of *latria*, and this is probably the real reason why the liturgy is in crisis, and why so many people seem incapable of taking part in liturgical prayer. But it is precisely this societal situation that makes celebration and feast salutary, indeed necessary, as a liberation from the bewitchment cast upon us by all those things our society finds plausible.[41] This is why a reduction of the Eucharist to its anthropological meaning would be a false aggiornamento of the church and of her liturgy. This affirmation is supported by the theological arguments we have adduced here. The glorification of God is the salvation of the human person; it is the sacramental form in which salvation is made present. This second goal of the Eucharist is thus not added on externally to the first but is essentially orientated to the first goal, in which it finds its own meaning. "The glory of God is the living human being."[42]

The Eucharist as Epiclesis
(Invocation of the Holy Spirit)

It goes without saying that thanksgiving, as the movement whereby the human person turns toward God, is
not a merit of his own, nor an independent,
autonomous achievement of the individual or of the
church as a whole. According to scripture, it is brought
about by the Spirit. It is, as it were, an *oratio infusa* by
means of which the grace which God has bestowed
flows back to the Creator.[43] Accordingly, an inherent
necessity makes the Eucharist an epiclesis, a request for
the sending of the Spirit so that he may bring about the
deeds of salvation that become a present reality in the
anamnesis. The epiclesis[44] is thus (so to speak) the
innermost soul of the Eucharist; it is in this sense that
the Eucharist, or more precisely the *prosphora* and *epiklēsis*
together, constitutes the form of the Lord's Supper.[45]

Ultimately, it is thanks to the biblical understanding
of the concept of *beraka* and *eulogia* or *eucharistia* that the
Eucharist has this character of a prayer for God's blessing—a character which is of central importance to the
Jewish prayers at mealtimes and to the Christian celebration of the Eucharist. This term denotes both God's
blessing on human beings and the act whereby human
beings bless God by praising his name.[46] This is why

Paul explicitly speaks of "the cup of blessing, over which we utter the blessing" (1 Cor 10:16).

This double significance of the Eucharist as a prayer for blessing and the gift of divine blessing helps us understand how a transformation in the meaning of the Eucharist could begin even in the earliest centuries, intensifying in the Middle Ages so that finally the Mass was no longer the ascent of human thanksgiving and adoration to God but a prayer beseeching the descent of his blessing. This transformation in the direction of the prayer is expressed very clearly when Isidore of Seville explains the term *eucharistia* as meaning *bona gratia*.[47] It was this understanding of the Eucharist as prayer and gift that generated the term "Mass," which subsequently came to be the dominant designation of the Eucharist. The original meaning is no doubt derived from *Ite, missa est,* the rite of dismissal linked to the closing blessing; this conclusion of the rite led to an understanding of the Mass in its totality as a blessing.[48] We should note that the Roman canon itself displays some of the characteristics of a solemn blessing.[49] Immediately after the preface—the prayer of thanksgiving in the strict sense—this canon prays: "Receive these holy and spotless sacrificial gifts and bless them," and immediately before the narrative of institution the priest says: "Give, O God, your blessing in fullness to these gifts." Although many people today find it hard to understand these benedictions, the Eucharist would lose its soul if they were removed: it would become a soulless action, purely external or at any rate purely human. This is why it is so good to see that the understanding of the Eucharist as the sacrament of God's gift has once more become a central dimension of today's ecumenical dialogue.[50]

According to scripture, it is the Holy Spirit who accomplishes the saving work of Jesus Christ in the world and in individual human beings. The Holy Spirit *is* the eschatological gift. This is why *pneuma* is the key concept in Paul's understanding of the Eucharist (cf. I Cor 10:3f.).[51] Following John 6:52ff. and I Cor 10:3f., the entire tradition is marked by the tension between the bodily and the spiritual reception of the sacrament,[52] and this aspect is made explicit by the epiclesis which prays for the coming of the Spirit both on the assembled community and on the gifts offered in sacrifice. The epicletic character attaches primarily to the Eucharist as a whole; all that the special epicleses inserted at various points and interpreted in various ways in the individual liturgical translations do is to make explicit this character of the entire Eucharist as prayer.[53] The epiclesis makes it clear that the Eucharist is not something over which the church (or the clergy) has power; nor is there anything automatic about the Mass, which is at once a humble and an authoritative prayer that the Holy Spirit may accomplish his work. Accordingly, the renewal of the epiclesis in the post-conciliar liturgy has immense importance, both in itself (as a matter of theological principle) and in the ecumenical context: not only in relation to the oriental churches, which attach a particular importance to the epiclesis (and where this has played a role in theological controversy over a long period),[54] but also in relation to the churches of the Reformation. Like the Latin liturgical tradition, these too have no explicit epiclesis; at the same time, however, they often accuse the Roman understanding of the Eucharist of an obsession with material and legal questions.[55]

When the epiclesis is given a prominent position, new light is shed on the sacrificial character of the Mass too, since this can help us to see more clearly that just as Jesus offered the sacrifice of the cross in the Spirit (Heb 9:14), so too the sacrifice of the Mass is a sacrifice in the Spirit, an *oblatio rationabilis,* as the liturgical texts say, echoing Rom 12:1 and 1 Pet 2:5.[56] This personalization and spiritualization of the Christian understanding of sacrifice must therefore ultimately be understood as a "pneumatologization," since it is the Spirit who bestows on us openness to God and to our fellow human beings. It is he alone who makes it possible for us to pray: "Abba, Father" (Rom 8:15; Gal

4:6), and hence it is he who (as the third eucharistic prayer puts it) makes us a gift pleasing to God.

The Eucharist as *Communio*

The Holy Spirit is sent out to accomplish the universal realization of the work of Jesus Christ and thus to integrate the world and history "in Christ." The goal of the Holy Spirit's activity in the Eucharist is thus *koinōnia* (*communio*) in and with Jesus Christ. This *communio* must be understood both in personal terms, as a participation in Christ and as the most utterly personal fellowship with him, and in ecclesial terms, as fellowship in Christ.[57] The goal and the fulfillment of the eucharistic celebration are personal and ecclesial *communio,* expressed in the kiss of peace (the *pax*) and in holy communion. Hence we may follow Augustine in calling the Eucharist the sign of unity and the bond of love.[58]

This aspect too is ultimately based on the institution of the Eucharist by Jesus in the context of a solemn meal held in common. The striking thing about this particular meal was Jesus' departure from normal custom when he gave the one cup to all those present, thus giving them all a share in himself and establishing the new covenant. The liturgical movement has often

inferred from this that the basic form of the Eucharist
is a meal,[59] a thesis that has sometimes led in liturgical
praxis to very arbitrary experiments, so that in extreme
cases—in direct opposition to what Paul writes in
I Cor 11:27ff.!—it is scarcely possible to distinguish
the Eucharist from an ordinary banquet or party. This
hypothesis fails to grasp the point that, although the
decisive and distinctive action of Jesus took place
within the framework of a meal, it also broke with the
customary form of a meal; and the repetition of the
special words and actions of Jesus began at a very early
date to be detached from the normal meal at which
nourishment was taken, as is clear both in Paul (I Cor
11:17-34) and in testimony from the second century.[60]
The same logic led to the celebration of the Eucharist
in the early morning.[61] When the Reformers called the
Eucharist the "Lord's Supper" (*Abendmahl* in German,
literally, "the evening meal"), they were doing something without precedent in liturgical history.[62] Instead
of speaking of the Eucharist in terms of a "meal," we
ought rather to speak of its "fellowship character" and
its ecclesial dimension.

Scripture emphasizes the connection between the
Eucharist and the church, for example, in the narratives
of the Lord's Supper, where Jesus speaks of the "blood
of the covenant" (Mark 14:24; Matt 26:28) or of the
"new covenant in my blood" (Luke 22:20; I Cor

11:25).[63] This makes the Eucharist a sign filled with the reality of the new age of salvation and of the new order of salvation. This new salvific reality affects both the relationship of the human person to God and our mutual relationships. Paul pursues this idea to its logical conclusion: he understands the sharing in the eucharistic body of the Lord as also a participation in the ecclesial body of Christ (I Cor 10:16f.). Accordingly, the church which celebrates the Eucharist is the new order of salvation.[64] No one has ever surpassed St. Augustine in the profundity of his understanding of this link. He went so far as to exclaim: "If you yourselves are the body of Christ and his members, then it is your own mystery that lies on the eucharistic table. . . . You should be what you see, and receive what you are!"[65]

In the course of the second eucharistic controversy in the eleventh century, the link between the sacramental body of Christ (which had been called the "mystical" body of Christ up to that time) and the ecclesial body of Christ was lost to view. In the debates of that period, the expression "mystical body of Christ" was misunderstood in a purely symbolic sense, leading people to speak instead of the "true" body of Christ; now, it was the church that began to be called the "mystical" body. This meant a very considerable loss of the awareness of the link between the Eucharist and the church.[66] Theologians of the stature of a Thomas Aquinas were still aware of these connections and expressed them with great vigor;[67] but taken as a whole, the outcome was a fatal individualization and privatization of the understanding and the praxis of the Eucharist.

This one-sided development was arrested only by the liturgical movement of the twentieth century—building on foundations laid by nineteenth-century theologians who had been influenced by the ideas of Romanticism (especially the ecclesiology of J. A. Möhler)—and by the Second Vatican Council. Now, the people of God in its liturgical assembly was once again understood as the subject of the eucharistic liturgy, and the "active participation" (*actuosa participatio*) of all those present was presented as the norm and ideal.[68] It is of course true that the "community Mass" (a term employed above all at the start of the liturgical movement) was so frequently presented as the antithesis of the so-called private Mass of the priest, which was now frowned upon, that people all too often overlooked the essential personal element, namely, the personal fellowship with Christ, which includes personal conversion and personal prayer, personal thanksgiving and adoration.[69] Earlier centuries would have called some of the ways in which the sacrament of the altar is administered and received today downright sacrilegious.[70] It is only too obvious that we have not yet succeeded in finding the correct equilibrium between personal and ecclesial *communio*.

The ecclesial dimension of the Eucharist is an important factor when we consider the question of admission to the eucharistic fellowship. An open celebration of the Lord's Supper to which one would invite not only the church but also the world seems on this basis impossible *a priori*.[71] As the sacrament of faith and the sign of unity, the Eucharist presupposes that those who take part are united in the common faith and in the one Baptism; the Eucharist brings about the purification, maturing, and deepening of this unity which already exists, and which the Mass in fact presupposes.[72] This reciprocity between Eucharist and church is constitutive for the question of eucharistic fellowship with those churches and ecclesial fellowships with which the Catholic Church does not have full ecclesial communion. As Catholics (and *a fortiori* the Orthodox) understand the Eucharist, this sacrament of unity presupposes that those who share in it also share in full ecclesial fellowship, which finds expression above all in fellowship with the local bishop and with the bishop of Rome as the one who carries out the Petrine ministry, which serves the unity of the church. This is why it is

not a matter of mere external ceremony when the
names of the local bishop and of the pope are men-
tioned in the canon of the Mass. This is an expression
of the *communio* within which alone the individual celebration of the Eucharist is meaningful—thanks to the
very nature of the Mass itself. This larger context helps
us to understand why the question of eucharistic fellowship becomes particularly acute when we pose the
question of the ordained ministry.[73] This latter question must not be seen in isolation but must be dis-
cussed in the total context of the Eucharist as *communio.*

This is why it would be exceedingly one-sided—
indeed, fatal—to reduce the question of the *communio*-
dimension of the Eucharist to the question of the
ministry.

Besides this, the *communio*-character of the Eucharist
has important ethical aspects.[74] The early church
already knew problems about fellowship in meals and
in the Eucharist between Jewish and Gentile Christians
(Antioch) and between the rich and the poor
(Corinth); today, similar conflicts abound worldwide.
It is certainly contrary to the nature of the Eucharist,
and contrary to the decisions of the early church on
this matter, to make the Mass a Eucharist for one particular race or class, whether one makes it the exclusive
celebration of the Eucharist for the privileged or a rev-
olutionary celebration of the underprivileged. But it is

just as great a failure to do justice to the essence of the Eucharist when one overlooks the ethical presuppositions and consequences of the celebration of the Mass in common: the *agape* which must be realized in concrete terms (cf. Matt 5:23f.), with the fulfillment of the demands of social justice as a minimum. One cannot share the eucharistic bread while refusing to share one's daily bread. It is not for nothing that the eucharistic assembly ends with words that send the worshipers out into the world. Assembling and being sent out are two poles that may not be divorced from one another or played off against each other: a mission without assembly becomes empty and hollow, but an assembly without mission becomes sterile and ultimately loses its credibility.

The Eucharist as Eschatological Sign

The eucharistic *communio* points beyond itself to the world and to the eschatological fulfillment of the world. This gives the Mass not only a social but also a universal, cosmic dimension. Here there is space only for a few introductory observations on this theme.[75]

For Jesus himself, the eschatological perspective plays a constitutive role in the celebration of the Last Supper (Mark 14:25 and parallels). Paul speaks explicitly of proclaiming the Lord's death "until he comes" (I Cor 11:26). This is why the community in Jerusalem broke bread day by day in anticipation of the eschato-logical joy (Acts 2:46). Joyful and solemn ceremonial is thus an essential element of the eucharistic celebration and ought not to be rejected *a priori* as pomp or triumphalism, nor should it fall victim to a joyless puri-tanism or a one-dimensional desacralization. This applies to church architecture and decoration, to church music, to the language used, the vestments, the rite, and so forth. The Eucharist should be celebrated in such a way that every element in it offers a foretaste of the coming kingdom of God.

The entire creation is drawn by means of the sacra-mental symbolism into the proleptic celebration and anticipation of the heavenly nuptial feast. When bread and wine, "fruit of the earth and work of human hands," are presented on the altar, there is a genuine anticipation of the eschatological glorification of God by all his creation, and the eschatological transforma-tion of the world is anticipated when these gifts are changed into the body and blood of Christ. This is why the good gifts of creation, which are filled with life and sanctified by means of Christ, are explicitly drawn into the great closing doxologies of the first, third, and fourth canons of the Mass. In this way, the Eucharist is the liturgy of the world (K. Rahner), the Mass of the world (P. Teilhard de Chardin).

The Eucharist—Synthesis of the Christian Mystery of Salvation

After setting out the various aspects of the Eucharist, let us conclude by asking: what is the Eucharist? Our answer can only be: the Eucharist makes present and synthesizes the entire Christian mystery of salvation in a sacramental manner. It embraces the creation and the eschatological new creation; it expresses both God's movement toward us human beings and the movement with which we respond to him, as individuals and as humankind. It is the comprehensive testament of the life, dying, and resurrection of Jesus Christ. It is the glorification of God and the salvation of the human person. It is personal and ecclesial, a gift that is given and a task that is assigned. Accordingly, it is impossible to understand the Eucharist on the basis of only one of its manifold aspects. It is not only—not even only primarily—a meal, or a thanksgiving and sacrifice. It is at one and the same time God's katabatic gift and the anabatic gift of self in sacrifice and thanksgiving, since it makes present Jesus Christ, his person and his work, and he is in his own person both the self-giving of God and the human gift of self in response to this.[76] But even this panoramic vision, inspired by Origen, is not sufficient. The all-decisive question is how we are to understand more precisely the unity of these two movements within the christological approach to the understanding of the Eucharist, for it is only the answer to this question that will reveal to us how the various aspects of the Eucharist form a unity. The God-man Jesus Christ is not a "compilation" of two separate elements (so to speak), namely, a divine and a human nature. Rather, the person of the Logos is the foundation of the subsistence of the human person of Jesus, who—precisely in virtue of the fact that he owes his existence to the Logos, and in virtue of the radical obedience by which he makes the gift of himself—is a true and perfected human being, indeed the "new" human being. In a manner analogous to this funda-mental christological affirmation, we may say that the katabatic and anabatic movements in the Eucharist are not merely juxtaposed without any inherent relation-ship: rather, they are mutually compenetrative. In a manner analogous to the Christ event, the bread and wine in the Eucharist, gifts of creation, are taken possession of in such a way that they lose their own autonomous substance, becoming pure signs: it is in this way that they symbolize sacramentally the sacrificial attitude of Jesus.[77] This in turn is brought about when the church is drawn in the Holy Spirit into Jesus' sacrificial attitude, thus becoming wholly one with him and in him. The three aspects of the Eucharist, which in scholastic theology are merely juxtaposed, without any hint at how they are mutually related—the eucharistic real presence, the Eucharist as sacrifice, and the Eucharist as sacrament—thus form one single, indissoluble, inherent unity. They are aspects of one totality, namely, the sacramental making-present of the one salvific mystery of Jesus Christ.

But we must go beyond even the christological perspective: the mystery of Jesus Christ can be understood only as the revelation of the trinitarian mystery, and the same is true of the Eucharist, which ultimately has a trinitarian structure (cf. SC 6). In the act of giving thanks, it addresses the Father, who is the source and origin of all being and of all salvation history; with thanksgiving, the church also receives in the Eucharist a gift God makes to human beings, namely, his self-communication in Jesus Christ, in order to be united to him in the most intimate fellowship (communion). Both of these are brought about in the power of the Holy Spirit, who prepares us for fellowship with Christ and makes this fellowship fruitful in a Christian life. Finally, the mutual self-communication and gift of self

of the persons of the Trinity are represented sacramentally and made present in the Eucharist. The trinitarian
profession of faith is the dogmatic summary of the
entire mystery of salvation, and the Eucharist is its
sacramental summary. Each in its own way is the creed
(*symbolum*) of the one mystery of salvation which God
accomplishes through Jesus Christ in the Holy Spirit.

This comprehensive understanding of the Eucharist
allows us to perceive the basic outlines of a eucharistic
spirituality. What we need is an utterly intimate union
of receiving and giving, of contemplation and action,
able to overcome the deadly antagonisms and conflicts
in today's church life—and not least, those conflicts
which threaten the understanding and the praxis of the
Eucharist itself. Such a eucharistic spirituality would
enable us to grasp how assembling to worship God and
being sent out into the world constitute a unity.

Eucharist—Sacrament of Unity

The Essential Connection between Eucharist and Church

What Is the *Res* of the Eucharist?

If we consult our traditional dogmatic handbooks, we will find very little—indeed, perhaps nothing at all—about the theme we shall discuss here: "Eucharist—sacrament of unity." The writers concentrate exclusively on the words of consecration, on the real presence, and on the sacrificial character of the Mass. If, however, we turn to scripture and read the works of the church fathers and the great scholastic theologians, we find a different and much more comprehensive picture. Naturally, this picture also includes the real presence of Christ in the Eucharist and the sacrificial character of the Mass, but they are situated within a larger context.

When Paul speaks of the Lord's Supper, he writes: "When you come together . . ." (I Cor 11:18, 20; cf. 14:26). He envisages the celebration of the Lord's Supper as an assembly. We find the same affirmation several times in the Letter to the Hebrews, and it is standard usage in the early church fathers. Accordingly, one of the most ancient names for the Eucharist is *synaxis,* a coming together, an assembly.[1] It is well known that the primary meaning of the Greek noun *ekklēsia,* as a translation of the Hebrew *qahal,* is "assembly."[2] If we combine these two observations, we may define the church as a eucharistic assembly. The church is to be found wherever Christians assemble around the table of the Lord to celebrate his Supper.

If we wish to appreciate the full nature of the Eucharist, in keeping with scripture and the fathers, we must begin by freeing ourselves from an individualistic understanding. This certainly does not mean that communion is something other than personal fellowship and unity with Jesus Christ; but in the Bible, in the early church, and in the tradition of the high Middle Ages, this fellowship and unity with Christ in the Eucharist are always seen in the larger context of the fellowship (*communio*) of the church. At a later date, people largely lost sight of the fact that the Eucharist is about fellowship. The individualism and subjectivism of the modern period left their mark on the average understanding of the Eucharist, and even more on eucharistic praxis. A change of course came only with the new movements in the church in the first half of the twentieth century, which received official recognition in the Second Vatican Council. This was, however, no innovation, but a return to the sources, a fresh reflection on the original tradition.

It was above all the great church father Augustine who understood the link between the Eucharist and the church in all its profundity, and who found wonderful expressions for this truth. He calls the Eucharist *signum unitatis, vinculum caritatis,* "sign of unity, bond of love,"[3] words that have imprinted themselves deeply on the memory of the church. They are quoted in full or in part in a whole series of conciliar texts: in the texts of the Fourth Lateran Council,[4] the Council of Trent,[5] and the Second Vatican Council (SC 47; LG 3; 7; 11; 26, and so forth). They are echoed in Thomas Aquinas too.[6] He knows the ancient name *synaxis* as a designation of the Eucharist,[7] which he calls *sacramentum ecclesiasticae unitatis,* "sacrament of ecclesiastical unity."[8]

Theologians such as Bonaventure and Thomas Aquinas do not consider this understanding of the Eucharist as sacrament of unity something trivial or arbitrary, the fruit of pious exaggeration, something that one might just be permitted to say *after* dealing with the dogmatic truths of the real presence and the sacrificial character of the Eucharist. On the contrary, this understanding is essential in their eyes: indeed, it is the essential truth about the Eucharist. The main point for Bonaventure and Thomas is not the presence of Jesus Christ in the Eucharist, which they consider only an intermediary reality. They call this *res et sacramentum,* that is, a "thing" which itself in turn is a sign pointing to the real "thing," and this real *res* of the Eucharist is the unity of the church.[9] The unity of the church is the reason why the Eucharist exists.

This first observation has a bearing on today's debate about the Eucharist: for if what we have stated is correct, then the crisis in the understanding of the Eucharist that affects some parts of the contemporary church is ultimately the heart of the crisis affecting the church as a whole. For this is not a crisis about one particular problem, still less a crisis about external reforms (which may in themselves be urgently necessary). The problem lies on a deeper level, and we must tackle it on the appropriate level by reflecting on the *res,* that is, the total meaning of the Eucharist and thereby on the total meaning of the church herself. We must free the Eucharist not only from a one-sided, individual understanding but also from a narrow and one-sided community perspective. We must give the Eucharist its proper place in the question about the unity of the church, which herself is a sign and instrument of unity with God and of unity and peace in the world (LG I).

Unity *Versus* Plurality

In order to understand this idea in all its depth and breadth, let us begin with a preliminary philosophical reflection: let us ask what "unity" actually means. This consideration can help us situate the Eucharist not only in the totality of the church but in reality as a whole.

The question of "the one" and "the many" has been a dominant problem ever since philosophical thinking began with Parmenides, Plato, and Aristotle. These thinkers see "the one" as the basis which makes "the many" possible and as the only criterion against which "the many" can be evaluated. This makes unity the foundation and the meaning of everything that exists, and this is why an axiom of scholasticism says, *ens et unum convertuntur.*[10] Thinkers in classical antiquity and in the high Middle Ages saw the whole of reality emerging in a great circular movement from "the one" and returning into unity at the end.[11]

When we speak of the Eucharist as the sacrament of unity, we must consider it against this all-embracing background, seeking to understand it in connection with the question of the meaning and basis of all that exists. The Eucharist would then be the Christian answer to the fundamental question about the meaning of reality as a whole.

For the tradition, this went without saying; but for us today, it has become problematic and suspect. Today, everyone talks about pluralism, which has become a basic concept in the description of the contemporary experience of reality. As such, the concept of pluralism is remarkably attractive and indeed convincing. One might say that the fundamental dogma of postmodern philosophy is that plurality is the only mode in which we have access to the totality. This philosophy is convinced that our thinking cannot probe behind the plurality of that which exists; indeed, one must refuse even to attempt to do so, for that would expose one to the suspicion of thinking in totalitarian terms.[12]

This generalized suspicion also casts suspicion on the link between the Eucharist and the unity of the church. As long ago as 1951, Ernst Käsemann put forward the thesis that the New Testament canon is the basis not of the unity of the church but of the plurality of Christian confessions.[13] This hypothesis could serve to justify an ecclesiological pluralism and relativism which would lead not only to a new emphasis on confessional differences but also to an ecclesiastical nationalism and to a provincialism on the part of the local churches.[14] The inference has often been drawn from this hypothesis that the various confessions need not unite; rather, they should recognize one another in their differences, indeed in their confessions of faith, which partly contradict one another. It is only logical that such an ecclesiological pluralism should dissolve the context in which the Eucharist stands: characteristically, we no longer hear of a unity in *communio*, but only of "intercommunion."

Philosophical and theological thinking has thus become a modest activity; it is not by chance that a philosopher such as G. Vattimo can describe it as *pensiero debole*, "weak thought." One is content to accept the de facto pluralism and refrains from examining the question of unity, the meaning of the totality, that which might be universally binding on all persons. One comes to terms with the plurality of the Christian confessions and refuses to strive for full *communio* and visible unity.

Such modesty fails to do justice not only to the heights of human thinking but also to the testimony of scripture and of the church's tradition, where unity is a fundamental category. For the Bible, conflict, division, and scattering abroad are the consequences of sin; they are the confusion of tongues as at Babel (Gen 11:7-9). The Bible reacts to this by offering the message of the one God, the one humankind, the one Redeemer, the one Spirit, the one Baptism, and the one church (cf. Eph 4:4-6).

The fundamental significance of the idea of unity is seen above all in the goal of the divine plan of salvation, namely, the eschatological gathering of Israel (Isa 40:11; Jer 23:3f.; 31:10; Ezek 34; 37) and the eschatological gathering of all the peoples (Isa 2:2-5; Mic 4:1-3; Ezek 37:16-28).[15] This means the overcoming of all conflicts between races, cultures, and religions. This eschatological gathering begins with the public ministry of Jesus and with his message of the coming of God's kingdom (Mark 1:14f. and parallels). Through his death, he tore down the dividing wall of enmity and established peace (Eph 2:14); in Christ, the old distinctions between Jews and Gentiles, slaves and free persons, men and women have lost their power to divide (Gal 4:28). Everything is to be recapitulated in Christ (Eph 1:10; Col 1:20). Thus God will be all in all at the end (1 Cor 15:28). The biblical name for this hope is *shalōm*.

The Universal Cosmic Dimension of the Eucharist

Jesus' proclamation of the kingdom of God (Mark 1:15 and parallels) was the very heart of all that he did here on earth, the star that guided him: God is to be "all in all."[16] It is against the background of this message about the kingdom of God that Jesus also celebrates the Last Supper. This interconnection between

the Eucharist and Jesus' proclamation of God's kingdom is obvious in all four accounts of the Last Supper
in the New Testament, since they all contain an eschatological look ahead to the coming kingdom of God.
In Mark's version, this perspective is formulated as follows: "Amen, I say to you, I shall no longer drink of the
fruit of the vine until that day on which I drink from
it anew in the kingdom of God" (Mark 14:25; cf. Matt
26:29; Luke 22:16; I Cor 11:26).

Even critical exegetes agree that the core of these
verses and the point that they are making go back to
the historical Jesus himself. These words show that
Jesus made a synthesis of his entire life on earth in the
event of the Last Supper, and at the same time looked
ahead to the fulfillment of all that exists. He understood the last meal he held with his disciplines against
an eschatological horizon. The earliest Christian community understood this eschatological dimension and
expressed it in the cry *Maranatha!* (I Cor 16:22; Rev
22:20; *Didache* 10:6). This is why (to borrow Alexander
Schmemann's phrase) the Eucharist is the sacrament of
the kingdom of God.

This cry for the second coming of Christ and the
hopeful expectation of his return transpose the
Eucharist into a universal cosmic dimension. Bread and
wine are the gifts of creation and the fruit of human
work; when they are brought into the eucharistic event,

the eschatological transformation of all reality is in a certain sense accomplished in them even now. This is why an important role is played in the eucharistic liturgy by lights, vestments, music, and all that human art can contribute. This has nothing to do with a desire for external ornaments, nor is it some cheap triumphalism; rather, the intention is to express the fact that the heavenly world penetrates our world and is present in it when the Eucharist is celebrated. The Letter to the Hebrews finds a convincing expression for this aspect: "You have come to Mount Zion, to the city of the living God, to the heavenly Jerusalem, to thousands of angels, to a solemn assembly, and to the fellowship of the firstborn whose names are written in heaven" (12:22f.).

This aspect is particularly important in the liturgy and theology of the Eastern churches.[17] In the postconciliar Western church, however, we have unfortunately become purists on this point, failing to demand high cultural standards. We have forgotten that cult and culture belong together and that the Eucharist is the anticipation of the eschatological praise which will be offered by the whole of creation. Since the Eucharist makes present the "heavenly Mass" (*missa caelestis*), it is also the "Mass of the world" (*missa mundi*), a proleptic realization of the heavenly glorification of God and of the eschatological perfecting of the world. In the

Eucharist, the world has once again become one in the praise of the Creator—and this means that the world has become whole. We must rediscover today this universal cosmic dimension of the Eucharist, and indeed of all the church's liturgy.[18]

We find similar ideas in a modern form in Pierre Teilhard de Chardin, above all in his "Mass on the World," a text he wrote in 1923 while he undertook research in the Ordos desert in China.[19] In an ecclesiastical situation in which a one-sidedly individualistic understanding had veiled the much more comprehensive doctrine put forward by the tradition, he discovered anew the cosmic dimension and the irradiation of the Eucharist. He did not confuse the transubstantiation in the strict sense of this word with the universal presence of the Logos; but he saw that the Eucharist indicates the direction to be taken by the cosmic movement, namely, the divinization of the world, which it anticipates.

We must recover this universal, cosmic dimension, refusing to be content with either the individualistic cut-down versions of the Eucharist or the modern reduction of the Mass to a narrow community perspective. This is necessary if we are to have a critical and constructive encounter with the ancient natural religions that are at home in Asia, Africa, and Latin America, and if we are to engage in a fruitful debate with neoreligious movements, such as New Age, which react critically to the anthropocentric understanding of reality (which has been dominant in the West during the modern period but is now in crisis) by promoting a natural-cosmic understanding of reality. This can be achieved only if we maintain with absolute firmness that the human person is the center and summit of all reality (GS 12), and this, of course, means nothing less than a serious reflection on the ontological foundations and presuppositions of theology. This is surely the most basic task of theology today.

The Eucharist as Sacrifice:
Fellowship under the Cross

This idea of the universal-cosmic dimension of the Eucharist must be taken onto a deeper level by means of one further perspective. The world in which we live is not whole and happy: our reality is marked by conflicts, where unity has been impaired and ruptured, and people cry out for healing and reconciliation. For us Christians, the salvation of the world stands under the sign of the cross. Christian art has expressed this relationship by combining the representation of the cross with that of the globe, either incising the cross on the globe or painting the globe on the cross.

This view of things is in keeping with the biblical

texts about the Lord's Supper. Jesus' last meal with his disciples is held on the eve of his suffering and death, and the cross already casts its proleptic shadow. This is why the accounts in Mark and Matthew place particular emphasis on the Old Testament ideas about sacrifice, interpreting what takes place at the Last Supper by recourse to the covenant made on Mount Sinai, when they speak of the "blood of the covenant" (Exod 24:8; Matt 26:28; Mark 14:24).

Although it is not a wholly straightforward matter for us today to understand such affirmations, this does not entitle us to follow Rudolf Bultmann in demythologizing them and interpreting them in terms of existentialism. These affirmations were made in the context of an all-embracing understanding of reality as sacred—an understanding shared by classical antiquity and by the Old Testament itself. The individual's guilt was seen as a disturbance of the sacred order of things, and as something that affected the entire community. This is why guilt represented a debt that had to be paid, that is, expiated. This was done by excluding the sinner from the community (which in practice meant his death), or else by transferring the guilt to an animal that died in his stead, thus restoring the sacred order of things that had been breached by human guilt.[20]

In the New Testament, especially in the texts about the Last Supper, the idea of vicarious representation in the fourth Song of the Servant of Yahweh in Deutero-Isaiah (Isa 52:13–53:12) is interpreted christologically: "This is my body for you" (I Cor 11:24; Luke 22:19), or in Mark and Matthew: "my blood poured out for the many" (Mark 14:24; Matt 26:28). "Body" here denotes the entire bodily existence; in the same way, "blood" is to be understood holistically as a designation of Jesus' life. Accordingly, the interpretative words of Jesus are saying: "This is myself, in the gift of my own self and of my life that I make for you and for all."

The apostle Paul uses very drastic language when he speaks of this voluntary vicarious death: Christ has become sin in our stead; he has become a curse; he has borne the curse that burdened us down (2 Cor 5:21; Gal 3:13). He takes upon himself all the history of disaster and guilt; he suffers voluntarily the vicious circle of sin that leads to hell and opens up the life that flows freely in the kingdom of God. His death is the victory of love over hatred and violence, the victory of obedience over the power of sin. This fundamentally alters the situation of the world.[21]

The New Testament texts that speak of the Last Supper employ a clear sacrificial terminology, and this makes it difficult to comprehend how it was possible in the past to deny the sacrificial character of the Eucharist, or how many people today can reduce it to a fraternal meal. The sacrificial character does not exclude the character of a fellowship meal; on the contrary, it is only the sacrificial character that explains how the Mass is a fellowship meal. According to the Old Testament, a fellowship in blood is created when the worshipers are sprinkled with blood and the covenant community is re-established. Sharing in the body which was given up for us establishes fellowship in the body of Christ, which is the church (1 Cor 10:16f.). Hence, sacrifice and unity belong together. The sacrifice aims at reconciliation and at restoring the unity that was lost. A fundamental text here is Eph 2:14, "For he is our peace, who has made us both one, and has broken down the dividing wall of hostility" through his death; cf. also 2 Cor 5:19, "In Christ, God was reconciling the world to himself, not counting their trespasses against them."

As is so often the case in theology, we must be on our guard against false alternatives here. The fact that the Eucharist is a community meal does not argue against its sacrificial character; and this, in turn, far from being antithetical to the dimension of community meal, is the very reason why the Mass is a community meal. Besides this, the sacrificial character preserves the Eucharist from banal trivialization, and only this dimension gives the Eucharist its true depth: for in this world, deformed as it is by sin, unity and peace cannot be achieved along any path other than that of forgiveness. If we were to abandon the sacrificial character of the Eucharist and its intimate link to the cross, we would also lose the seriousness which is inherent in its character as fellowship meal. Eucharistic community means community under the cross.

At this point, we once again encounter a weakness of the postconciliar development. The affirmation that unity and fellowship are possible only under the sign of the cross entails that the Eucharist as sacrament of unity is not possible without the sacrament of forgiveness, the sacrament of penance. The ancient church was fully aware of this relationship; in the early centuries, the visible form of the sacrament of penance consisted in the readmission of the sinner to eucharistic fellowship. An intimate link existed between *communio, excommunicatio,* and *reconciliatio.*[22]

It may indeed be the case that this link between the sacraments of penance and the Eucharist was sometimes understood too narrowly in the period before the Second Vatican Council, but we must ask ourselves today whether we still take seriously the exhortation in the Sermon on the Mount to seek reconciliation with our brother before going to the altar of God (Matt 5:23f.), and whether we do not pass too lightly over Paul's warning that we must distinguish between the eucharistic bread and ordinary bread, lest we eat and drink unworthily (I Cor 11:27). Both these admonitions are also important in the ecumenical context, for there can be no unity among the Christian churches without conversion and renewal.[23]

Dietrich Bonhoeffer, the Lutheran theologian executed by the Nazis in 1945, warned rightly against "cheap grace" and a cheap Eucharist: "Cheap grace means grace at knock-down prices . . . a sacrament at knock-down prices. . . . Cheap grace is Baptism without community discipline, the Lord's Supper without the confession of sins, absolution without personal confession." Bonhoeffer sees cheap grace as the reason for the catastrophic situation the church is in.[24] The rediscovery and renewal of the understanding of the Eucharist as assembly and fellowship meal were certainly important, and no sensible person would wish to turn back the clocks to an earlier period; but a superficial understanding, which averts its gaze from the cross and from penance, trivializes these two aspects and ultimately leads to the eucharistic crisis that we can perceive in many areas of the church's life today.

The Intimate Connection between the Eucharist and the Church

After laying these foundations, let us now speak of the intimate connection between the Eucharist and the church. It has often been denied that the church has any basis at all in Jesus' own actions and in the message he proclaimed; this is because of the lasting impact made by the individualistic understanding of Jesus' message about the kingdom of God, as formulated in the celebrated lectures held by Adolf von Harnack in 1900: "The kingdom of God comes by coming to individuals, entering their souls, and taking hold of them. . . . Here, every dramatic element in the external sense of events in world history has disappeared, and all external future hope has likewise sunk without trace."[25]

A number of different developments helped overcome this individualistic understanding and brought to light again the community character of Christianity and of the Eucharist. Here we may mention the emphasis laid on the community by neo-Romanticism (Romano Guardini), with the related Slavophile ecclesiology of *sobornost* (A. Khomiakov); in this connection, Johann Adam Möhler too played an influential role. The most important factor, however, was the rediscovery of the theology of the church fathers (Henri de Lubac), and not least the reading of sacred scripture itself.

The most significant scriptural testimony against the individualistic view is the fact that Jesus chose the twelve in a special manner from the larger circle of those who were his disciples, and that he appointed (or literally, "created"; *epoiēsen* in Greek) them as such (Mark 3:13-19 and parallels). Jesus understood himself as the shepherd promised by the prophets who would gather together the lost sheep of Israel (Mark 6:34; John 10). Accordingly, the appointment of the twelve is a symbolic prophetic action which makes it clear that Jesus intends to gather together the people of God. As representatives of the eschatological people of God, the twelve take part in the last meal, at which Jesus also looks ahead to the future of the community of disciples after his death (Mark 14:25 and parallels) "until he comes" (1 Cor 11:26).

This is why the young community regularly comes together for the breaking of the bread after Jesus' death and resurrection and after the outpouring of the Spirit (Acts 2:46). This unanimous coming together *epi to auto* ("in the same place") is a fundamental activity which is characteristic of the young church (Acts 2:1, 44, 47). Paul too uses the expression *epi to auto* when he speaks of the church's coming together to celebrate the Eucharist (1 Cor 11:18, 20), and it has already become a technical term by the time of Ignatius of Antioch.[26]

From the very beginning, then, the eucharistic assembly and the church were intimately linked, as we also see in the fact that the four accounts of the Last Supper show clear traces of liturgical stylization: in other words, they tell us not only about the last meal that

Jesus held with his disciples, but also about the eucharistic meals of the early church. There was never any early period of the church without the Eucharist. From the outset, the church understood herself as a eucharistic assembly.

In his First Letter to the Corinthians, Paul reflects explicitly on the intimate connection between the church and the Lord's Supper. He teaches that we are already received into the one body of Christ by means of Baptism (Rom 6:3-5; I Cor 12:12f.; Gal 3:27f.), and he makes a similar affirmation about our sharing in the one eucharistic chalice and the one eucharistic bread: "The cup of blessing which we bless, is it not a participation in the blood of Christ? The bread which we break, is it not a participation in the body of Christ? Because there is one bread, we who are many are one body, for we all partake of the one bread" (I Cor 10:16f.).

Paul writes here that the sharing (*koinōnia, participatio*) in the one chalice and the one bread gives us a share in the death and resurrection of Christ and binds us to one another so that we form the one body of the Lord, which is the church. The Eucharist does not institute this fellowship, since it presupposes the fellowship which has already been bestowed by Baptism; rather, the Eucharist actualizes, renews, and deepens it. In this sense, sharing in the one eucharistic body of Christ brings about sharing in the one ecclesial body of Christ and the ecclesial fellowship which unites Christians.[27]

This Pauline text has left a profound imprint on the consciousness of the church. The church fathers in the East and the West never tire of proclaiming that the Eucharist is the sacrament of unity; they return to this theme again and again, taking up the affirmation of the *Didache* (9:4): "As the bread was scattered on the hills and brought together to form one bread, so let your church be gathered together from the ends of the earth into your kingdom."[28]

The most celebrated words are those of St. Augustine, already quoted: the Eucharist is the sacrament of unity and the bond of love. These words are repeated by Thomas Aquinas, in many documents of the ecclesiastical magisterium, and in the texts of the Second Vatican Council.[29] According to Augustine, it is by the power of the Eucharist that the church is made one.[30] For "the sharing in the body and blood of Christ brings about nothing other than this: that we are transferred into that which we receive" (Leo the Great).[31] Thus, eucharistic fellowship and ecclesial fellowship belong indissolubly together. This is the common tradition of the church in East and West.

Sadly, this interconnection was largely forgotten in the aftermath of the second eucharistic controversy in the eleventh century. Henri de Lubac has traced the

history of this development.[32] Up to that point, theologians had spoken of the threefold body of Christ:
the historical, the mystical (i.e., eucharistic), and the
ecclesial body. The symbolic understanding of the
Eucharist proposed by Berengar of Tours meant,
however, that the designation of the Eucharist as the
"mystical body of Christ" came to be open to misunderstanding, as if the term was meant in a purely
symbolic sense. Accordingly, the Eucharist was now
called the "real body of Christ," and the term "mystical body" was applied to the church. Now, however, the
word "mystical" was no longer derived (as hitherto)
from *mystēria/sacramenta,* nor was the church understood
as the body that is built up by means of the *mystēria,*
that is, the sacraments; rather, the term was understood
in the sense of a spiritual or even merely moral and
societal body, referring to Christendom at that period.
This entailed a dissociation of Eucharist and church:
the Eucharist was individualized and the church politi-
cized.

As we have seen, great theologians such as Bonaventure and Thomas Aquinas were still aware of the connection between the Eucharist and the church, and this
perspective remains alive even as late as the early writings of Martin Luther.[33] But it is only in the twentieth
century that the holistic view once again came into its

own. It finds expression in many texts of the Second Vatican Council, and Pope John Paul II repeats it emphatically in his encyclical *Ecclesia de eucharistia* (2003). The church is not something we "make" and organize. It is the Eucharist that makes the church, just as it is the church that celebrates the Eucharist.[34]

This means *ubi eucharistia, ibi ecclesia*, "Wherever the Eucharist is celebrated, there is the church." The Eucharist is not just one sacrament among others, it is the *sacramentum sacramentorum*,[35] the source, center, and summit of the life of the church.[36] In it, the entire mystery of our salvation finds its synthesis.[37] The proposition *ubi eucharistia, ibi ecclesia* has become the fundamental principle of the modern eucharistic ecclesiology, which is not only found in Orthodox theologians but is also echoed in various ways in a number of texts of the Second Vatican Council[38] and in postconciliar Catholic theologians. For example, the decree on ecumenism affirms that the church of God is built up and grows in the local churches by means of the Eucharist, and that this fellowship is made visible by means of concelebration (UR 15).

This insight has consequences for the way in which we understand the church and her unity. Since the church is there wherever the Eucharist is celebrated, no community that celebrates the Mass can isolate itself and withdraw complacently into itself; it can celebrate the Eucharist only in *communio* with all the other communities that celebrate the Eucharist. Hence, the eucharistic ecclesiology is the basis not of the independence of the local churches but of their interdependence, or more precisely, of their *perichoresis*, that is, their mutual compenetration.[39] Accordingly, the recent ecclesiology of *communio* understands the unity of the church as a unity of *communio*.[40] Her unity is not the result of a logically posterior unification of local churches; nor do the local churches come into being by derivation from the universal church. The unity of the church is not to be understood on the lines of an empire or of a federation: it is a reality *sui generis.* Just as the universal church exists only in and out of local churches, so the local churches in turn exist only in and out of the universal church (cf. LG 23).

When we look at the details of how this *communio*-unity is understood, we see clear divergences between the Catholic, the Orthodox, and especially the Protestant positions, which become most acute where the Petrine ministry of the pope is concerned; we cannot discuss these problems here. But even within the Catholic Church itself, we find different evaluations of the relationship between the universal and the local church. Historically speaking, the path taken by the church led from the *communio*-ecclesiology of the first millennium to the unity-ecclesiology of the second millennium.[41] The Second Vatican Council rediscovered the significance of the local church,[42] thereby providing an impetus for a new development in the third Christian millennium. The goal of this development is a unity that unambiguously excludes all contradictions but regards a plurality of cultures, languages, rites, and customs in the church not as a defect but as a valued treasure.

This theme of unity and plurality does not only concern the church on the level of general principles; it is actualized in every celebration of the Eucharist, in which the various charisms, spiritual movements, and communities celebrate together and in which the differences between men and women, poor and rich, masters and slaves, educated and uneducated lose (or ought to lose) their importance, where all receive (or ought to receive) the same welcome and respect (I Cor 11:18-22; Jas 2:1-7), and where all share (or ought to share; Acts 2:44f.).

This is why collections of money for the poor have been taken up in the community assemblies from the very origins of the church (Acts 11:29; Gal 2:9f.; I Cor 16:1-4; 2 Cor 8–9). We cannot share the eucharistic bread while refusing to share our daily bread. Paul goes one step further, when he applies to the ministry of love and of fellowship, which is made concrete in the collection of money, the term "liturgy" (*leitourgia*), which in turn leads to an outpouring of thanksgiving to God (Rom 15:27; 2 Cor 9:12f.). He employs a concept here that had a social-political and a cultic sense both in classical antiquity and in Judaism, and which was understood as the symbolic fulfillment of the promised pilgrimage of all the peoples of the world to Zion.[43] In this social sense, too, the Eucharist is the sacrament of unity.[44] But this eucharistic root of the church's social teaching still awaits further examination and elaboration.

Eucharist and Ecumenism

Our reflections on unity and plurality have brought us to the theme of ecumenism, on which we shall concentrate in the last part of this essay. We have already seen clearly that the question of the church's unity is not a minor problem nor a luxury that we might perhaps grant ourselves once we had achieved all our "important" ecclesial aims. On the contrary, unity is a fundamental category of the Bible and the explicit charge that Jesus gives his disciples. Jesus wanted only one church. On the evening before he suffered, he bequeathed us, as his own testament, the prayer and the active concern for unity (John 17:21). Accordingly, we must carry out this commission of the Lord to seek unity, without looking for immediate results.

Pope John Paul II has put it clearly: "Believing in Christ means wanting unity."[45] Thus, ecumenism is not some trivial issue, nor an optional extra;[46] it is the path of the church.[47] We may say of ecumenism what we have said of the church as a whole: just as one cannot "make" and organize the church, so one cannot "make" and organize ecumenism, which is not our work, but an impulse of the Holy Spirit (UR 1; 4). It is he alone who can give us the greater ecumenical unity. Accordingly, ecumenism is not a political, diplomatic, or purely pragmatic undertaking. It is primarily a spiritual concern. Its goal, namely, visible unity, means in concrete terms that we are able to gather together around the one table of the Lord, sharing in the one eucharistic body of Christ and drinking from the one chalice.

For the sake of the truth, it is not possible in today's situation for all Christians to gather around the one table of the Lord and partake of his one Supper, and this is a deep wound on the body of the Lord—and, ultimately, a scandal. We cannot simply accept this. The Eucharist, as a "mystery of faith," presupposes the unity of the church. Since, however, we already possess a real though not yet perfect fellowship, thanks to the one Baptism that we have all received, we are in a kind of intermediary situation. Here, we must also distin-

guish between the Eastern churches, which have preserved a fully valid Eucharist and which we therefore
acknowledge as churches in the full sense (UR 15), and
those ecclesial communities which have not preserved
the original and total reality of the eucharistic mystery
(UR 22).

In order to cope properly with this very complicated
intermediary situation, the council proposed two principles (UR 8). First of all, Eucharist and unity belong
together. One receives the Eucharist in that church fellowship to which one belongs; this is a fundamental
principle laid down in the early church, and we cannot
change this rule. This is why we as Catholics cannot
issue a general, open invitation to the Eucharist, nor
practice "eucharistic fellowship." At the same time,
however, the council is familiar with a second principle:
salus animarum suprema lex ("the highest law is the salvation of souls": canon 1752). The unity of the church
is not a totalitarianism that would "absorb" individuals
and subjugate them with ruthless force to an abstract
ideology of unity: rather, the individual is taken seriously in his unique personal situation, which is not to
be regarded as merely one instance of some general
principles. This is why the church acknowledges the
possibility of individual solutions under certain circumstances.[48] Indeed, the pope has written that he
rejoices that in particular individual cases, Catholic

priests are permitted to administer this sacrament to other Christians.[49]

We cannot discuss all the details of these regulations here. Taken as a whole, they seem to me an appropriate response to our contemporary situation. They give each bishop sufficient freedom of movement to let him reach prudent pastoral decisions in specific individual instances. Ultimately, this is a spiritual question, and spiritual questions cannot be regulated by canon law alone. We need pastoral wisdom and the discernment of spirits (I Cor 12:10; I Thess 5:21; I John 4:1).[50]

We must do more than simply draw up a list of all those things that we unfortunately cannot yet do. Rather, we must reflect on what we in fact can do and ought to do in order to achieve full eucharistic *communio*. The basis of these reflections is the conviction that the unity of the church is a gift of the Holy Spirit, which has been bestowed on the church and which she cannot lose: human guilt does not have the power to destroy it. This is why this unity is a reality—not only a goal toward which we must make our way, still less something that will exist only in the *eschaton*. As Catholics, we are convinced that the church of Jesus Christ and her unity "subsist" in the Catholic Church.[51]

This is why the future, more comprehensive ecumenical unity will not be another church, or a new church; rather, it will take its place within the trajectory already carved out by the tradition. The greater ecumenical unity for which we hope will be the "old" church, indeed—but the "old" church in a new form.

The tradition is not something mechanical, and the faith is not handed on as one passes a dead coin from hand to hand. As Johann Adam Möhler and John Henry Newman taught, the tradition is alive, sustained and filled by the Holy Spirit (DV 8). Through the Holy Spirit, the church is introduced ever anew into the fullness of the truth (John 16:13). It is the Spirit who preserves her continually in the freshness of her youth.[52] This is why we cannot employ the tradition in order to set up immovable obstacles along the path where the Holy Spirit wishes to lead the church. On the contrary, on her path through history, the church always needs purification and renewal in the Holy Spirit (LG 8).

This renewal takes place in many ways, including the ecumenical dialogue, which, of course, must not be confused with a relativism on questions of dogma or a willingness to sell off our own tradition cheaply.[53] We must be on our guard against cheap grace—and against cheap ecumenism. The point of ecumenical dialogue is not that we should abandon our own identity but that we should let it be purified, grow, and mature. Ecumenical dialogue entails the examination of one's own conscience[54] and an exchange of gifts[55] in which we learn from those gifts that the Holy Spirit has brought about in the other churches and ecclesial communities (LG 15; UR 3) in order to move beyond the still imperfect *communio* to full *communio.*

In the last few decades, we Catholics have learned a great deal from our Protestant brothers and sisters about the significance of the Word of God and the interpretation of the Bible, and this has enriched our ecclesial life and spirituality. Now, our Protestant friends are learning from us about the significance of the liturgy and the sacraments. This means that we are drawing closer to one another not on the level of the lowest common denominator; on the contrary, we are drawing closer together by means of a genuine mutual enrichment. In this way, along the path of ecumenism, the church can become concretely and fully what she always was and what she remains; the ecumenical dialogue is meant to help her bring about the concrete realization of her own catholicity in all its fullness (UR 4).

This is a difficult path; doubtless, the journey will not be short. But it is a salutary and necessary process, to which there is no alternative in theological or in practical terms, since the divisions among Christians are one of the greatest hindrances to the fulfillment of the commission Jesus gave us to bring his good news to the world. The church's unity is not an end in itself; it is orientated to the great goal "that the world may believe" (John 17:21). This is why ecumenism and world mission are intimately linked; the success of each depends, in fact, on the other.

Even externally, this can be seen in the word "ecumenism" itself, since the original meaning of the Greek *oikoumenē* is the entire inhabited earth. The deeper internal link lies in the Eucharist. Just as ecumenism aims at eucharistic table fellowship, so the deeper inherent reason for the church's mission lies in the eucharistic mystery, in Jesus' gift of his life "for the many."[56]

In the ecumenical and missionary movements, the church grows in history toward her eschatological fullness. On the path of mission, she spreads out and welcomes into herself the entire riches of the peoples and of their cultures; in the ecumenical movement, she lets herself be enriched by the gifts and the spiritual experiences of the other churches and ecclesial communities. In ecumenism and in mission, she grows to the full stature of Christ (Eph 4:13).[57]

Thus both ecumenism and mission are decisive for the future shape of the church. This will be a unity in immense plurality, since church unity does not mean church uniformity. At the same time, of course, church unity does not mean the peaceful coexistence of mutu-

ally contradictory positions, since such an ecclesiological pluralism, an intercommunion without *communio* in
the one truth, in the same sacraments, and in fellowship
with the one apostolic ministry would be dishonest, a
"unity" without any *genuine* unity. But true unity and the
full *communio* which is based on the *communio* with the
triune God (I John I:3) are a deep mystery which can
be portrayed only by means of the great wealth of
complementary forms of expression. Only as this kind
of unity in plurality is the church the quasi-sacramen-
tal form of the "manifold wisdom" of God (Eph 3:10)
and the icon of the one God in three Persons (LG 4;
UR 2).

Our conclusion thus brings us back to our starting
point. Both the ecumenical movement and the church's
mission are sustained by the same vision, which experiences a proleptic realization in every celebration of the
Eucharist, namely, the eschatological gathering of all
peoples, all languages and cultures, in the common
praise of God. Along the path of ecumenism and of
mission, the church is meant to draw closer to this goal
of God's salvific plan. The goal of ecumenism, that all
the disciples of Christ should assemble around the one
table of the Lord, sharing in the one bread and drinking from the one cup, belongs to God's great plan of
salvation.[58] Along the path of ecumenism and of mission, the church is meant to become in a concrete and

convincing manner what she already is, in terms of her very being: a sacrament (so to speak), that is, a sign and instrument of unity and of peace in the world (LG 1). The Eucharist is the sacrament of this unity.

"Peace be with you!" (John 20:19). This greeting of the risen Jesus rings out in every celebration of the Mass. In every Eucharist, we exchange the kiss of peace and pray for unity and for peace. Every celebration of the Eucharist is a feast of peace, bearing witness to our conviction that Jesus Christ "is our peace" (Eph 2:14). He is the peace of the world.

Abbreviations

Document of the First Vatican Council

DF   *Dei Filius,* dogmatic constitution on the
Catholic faith

Documents of the Magisterium of the Second Vatican Council

CD   *Christus Dominus,* decree on the pastoral ministry of bishops in the church

DV   *Dei Verbum,* dogmatic constitution on divine revelation

GS   *Gaudium et spes,* pastoral constitution on the church in today's world

LG   *Lumen gentium,* dogmatic constitution on the church

PO   *Presbyterorum ordinis,* decree on the ministry and life of priests

SC   *Sacrosanctum concilium,* dogmatic constitution on the sacred liturgy

UR   *Unitatis redintegratio,* decree on ecumenism

Other Documents

DH   "Denzinger-Hünermann": Heinrich Denzinger,
      Enchiridion symbolorum definitionum et declarationum de
      rebus fidei et morum, rev. ed. Peter Hünermann, ed.
      Freiburg, Basle, and Vienna, 2001.

Notes

Chapter 1: The Celebration of the Eucharist and the Worshiping Life of the Communities

This essay is based on my pastoral letter "Die Feier der Eucharistie" ("The Celebration of the Eucharist"), addressed to the parishes of the diocese of Rottenburg-Stuttgart on May 21, 1998: *Kirchliches Amtsblatt der Diözese Rottenburg-Stuttgart* (= *KABl*) (1998): 96-104; cf. also "Die Feier der Eucharistie—Fest des neuen Lebens" ("The Celebration of the Eucharist—Feast of New life"), a letter to the parishes of the diocese of Rottenburg-Stuttgart in Lent 1996: *KABl* (1996): 13-16; "Eucharistiefeier und Wortgottesdienst an Sonn- und Feiertagen" ("Celebration of the Eucharist and Liturgy of the Word on Sundays and Holy Days"): *KABl* (1996): 123-25.

1. The publication of the instruction *Ecclesiae de mysterio,* on the participation of the laity in the ministry of priests (1997), generated a vigorous discussion of many specific questions; the pastoral letter I issued as bishop of Rottenburg-Stuttgart in 1998 sought to provide an orientation on some of these questions. The instruction *Ecclesiae de mysterio* has often been misunderstood. It does not intend to speak of the dignity and mission of the laity on a fundamental theological level; this had already been done in detail in the apostolic exhortation *Christifideles laici* (1988). The instruction restricts its attention to the much more limited sphere of those

laity who, thanks to a special commission, take part in specific tasks of the ordained ministry, and its concern is to avoid blurring the distinct profiles of the priestly ministry (on the one hand) and of those ministries (on the other hand) for which laypersons can be commissioned in this way—for such a confusion would profit no one. Accordingly, the instruction does not seek to deprive the laity of anything that is theirs on the basis of Baptism and confirmation; equally, it wishes to ensure that the priest too is not deprived of anything that is his on the basis of his priestly ordination. This does not mean that the Roman text posits a gulf between priests and laity. Rather, it wishes to preserve the unity in the multiplicity of gifts and tasks in the church. This is one of scripture's central concerns and finds particularly prominent expression in Paul's image of the church as one body with many members (1 Cor 12:4-31).

2. Important and authoritative sources are the following documents: Second Vatican Council, Constitution on the Liturgy *Sacrosanctum Concilium*; John Paul II, *Apostolic Letter on the Twenty-Fifth Anniversary of the Constitution on the Liturgy "Sacrosanctum Concilium"* (1988); Catechism of the Catholic Church (1993). The "General Introduction" to the Roman Missal is also very helpful. All these documents furnish reliable and authoritative information about what the Catholic faith teaches about the Eucharist and the liturgy.

3. Many valuable books provide further education in liturgy and can be recommended for personal reading. The dioceses have liturgical commissions which publish practical guides and are happy to provide useful advice.

4. Grave reasons that dispense one from participation in the

Eucharist can, for example, be illness, the frailty of old age, obligations of love of one's neighbor (e.g., the care of seriously ill family members or looking after small children), indispensable professional obligations (e.g., for those working in hospital care or in the service sector), or the fact that no Eucharist is celebrated where one lives (cf. canon 1248 §2).

5. See below the section "The Significance of Celebrations of the Word of God."

6. LG 33; AA 24; canons 230 §3; 910 §2.

7. The essential guidelines for cooperative pastoral activity in the diocese of Rottenburg-Stuttgart are provided by the "Pastoral Perspectives" (1992) and "Community Leadership in a Time of Transition" (1997). These two texts are not affected by the Roman instruction *Ecclesiae de mysterio,* since this text itself likewise pleads for the concept of cooperative pastoral work. This means that the two fundamental texts have remained in force in the diocese even after 1998.

8. In view of this universal Christian tradition on which the binding formulation in canon law is based, it is impossible for the diocese of Rottenburg-Stuttgart to strike out on a path all of its own. See the decree of Bishop Georg Moser on the regulation of preaching by laypersons: *KABl* (1986): 132. All the diocesan regulations about full-time stipendiary lay pastoral ministers envisage that these persons are commissioned to preach "in keeping with ecclesiastical regulations."

9. Without making any claim to present an exhaustive list, I mention as examples: parish catechesis and religious instruction in school; preaching in celebrations of the Word of God; addresses during Vespers, Baptisms, funerals, and other occa-

sional rites; an introduction to the celebration of the Eucharist; sermons in Advent and Lent; and holding lectures on religious subjects.

10. SC 35, 4; pastoral letter of Bishop Georg Moser on "Sunday Worship—Even When No Priest Is Present," *KABl* (1977): 181-83.

Chapter 2: Recognizing Jesus in the Breaking of the Bread

1. *Didache* 14:1; Ignatius of Antioch, *Letter to the Ephesians* 5:2f.; 13:1; *Letter to the Philadelphians* 6:2; *Letter to the Magnesians* 7:1f.; 9:1; Justin, *First Apology* 67:3; Tertullian, *Apology* 39:2.

2. *Letter to the Magnesians* 9:1.

3. Pliny the Younger, *Letters* 10:96.

4. Patrologia Latina 8:707, 709f.; quoted by Pope John Paul II, apostolic letter *Dies Domini* (1998) 46.

5. Leo the Great, *Second Sermon on the Ascension* 61.

6. *Letter to Diognetus* 5.

Chapter 3: The Presence of Jesus Christ in the Eucharist

1. Augustine, *Confessions* I:1.

2. We cannot discuss here the question of the presence of "seeds" of the reality of Christ in other religions and their cultures, nor the question of how those who do not believe in Jesus Christ can be saved.

3. The scholastic concept of "substance" does not refer to what we today understand as "substance" and "substances," that

is, a material reality. The substantial presence of Christ in the Eucharist is not to be understood in material terms, but on the analogy of spiritual realities.

4. This is the teaching of the Council of Trent (DH 1636). When the Greek fathers call the Eucharist "symbol, image, equal image, *typos*," they are using these terms to denote something filled with the reality of Christ (cf. J. Betz, *Die Eucharistie in der Zeit der griechischen Väter*, I/I [Freiburg im Breisgau, 1955], 217-42). Basically, the later doctrine of transubstantiation does not intend to affirm anything different from this sacramental understanding of the Eucharist.

5. In the dialogue with Protestant Christians, the primary question is who may preside at the celebration of the Eucharist, and more precisely the question of the ordained ministry and of the episcopal ministry in the apostolic succession.

6. The exposition of this link by Matthias Joseph Scheeben, *Die Mysterien des Christentums*, new ed. by J. Höfer (Freiburg im Breisgau, 1951), 385-441, has lost nothing of its authoritative character.

7. Ignatius of Antioch, *Letter to the Smyrnaeans* 7:1; cf. 2:1; 4:2; 5:2; *Letter to the Trallians* 10:1.

8. Literal translation of the Latin text: *Adoro te devote, latens Deitas, quae sub his figuris vere latitas. . . . Visus, tactus, gustus in te fallitur, sed auditu solo tuto creditur* (Thomas Aquinas).

9. *Tibi se cor meum totum subiicit, quia te contemplans totum deficit* (Thomas Aquinas).

10. Naturally, this does not entail any lessening of the significance of the eucharistic veneration and adoration which developed in the Latin church during the second millennium, for this form of prayer is, as it were, an echo of the celebration of

eucharistia and *eulogia.* However, as the Council of Trent affirmed, the goal and the fulfillment of eucharistic devotion is "eating": *ut sumatur institutum* ("in order that that which was instituted may be consumed," DH 1643).

11. Cyril of Jerusalem, *Mystagogical Catecheses* 4:3.

12. Cyril of Alexandria, *Commentary on the Gospel of John* 10:2.

13. Ignatius of Antioch, *Letter to the Ephesians* 20:2.

14. Irenaeus of Lyons, *Against the Heresies* IV 8:5; cf. V 2:2.

15. *Didache* 9:5; 10:6; 14:1; Justin, *First Apology* 66; Augustine, *Commentary on John's Gospel* 26:11.

16. We find a very beautiful and profound interpretation of the custom of receiving communion in the hand in Cyril of Jerusalem, *Mystagogical Catecheses* 5:21: the communicant lays one hand over the other, thus forming a throne to receive the king.

Chapter 4: Ecumenism of Life and Eucharistic Fellowship

1. John Paul II, encyclical on the church's missionary activity, *Redemptionis missio* 57.

2. See the convergence document on "Baptism, Eucharist, and Ministry" (the Lima declaration), published by the Commission for Faith and Order of the World Council of Churches in 1982; the document on "The Lord's Supper," produced by a joint Roman Catholic and Evangelical Lutheran commission (1979); the Common Statement on Justification (1999); and many other texts.

3. First Vatican Council, constitution on the Catholic faith, *Dei Filius,* DH 3020.

4. John Paul II, encyclical on ecumenism, *Ut unum sint* 28; 57.

5. Canon 844; instruction *Redemptionis sacramentum* 85.

6. *Ut unum sint* 46.

7. John Paul II, encyclical on the Eucharist *Ecclesia de eucharistia* 46.

8. John Paul II, *Novo millennio ineunte* 43.

Chapter 5: Sacrament of Unity—Plurality of Aspects

This essay was first published under the title "Einheit und Vielfalt der Aspekte der Eucharistie. Zur neuerlichen Diskussion um Grundgestalt und Grundsinn der Eucharistie," *IKaZ Communio* 14 (1985): 196-215. It was reprinted in my book *Theologie und Kirche* (Mainz, 1987), 300-320. The bibliographical references in the present publication are those of the original article.

1. This is not the appropriate place to present the enormous amount of scholarly work devoted to this question or to discuss individual exegetical details. For an overview of biblical scholarship, see H. Lessig, "Die Abendmahlsprobleme im Lichte der neutestamentlichen Forschung seit 1900" (diss., Bonn, 1953); E. Schweizer, "Das Herrenmahl im Neuen Testament. Ein Forschungsbericht," in idem, *Neotestamentica* (Zurich and Stuttgart, 1963), 344-70; H. Patsch, *Abendmahl und historischer Jesus* (Stuttgart, 1972); F. Hahn, "Zum Stand der Erforschung des urchristlichen Herrenmahls," *Evangelische Theologie* (= *EvTh*) 35 (1975): 553-63; H. Feld, *Das Verständnis des Abendmahls*, Beiträge zur Forschung 50 (Darmstadt, 1976), 4-76.

2. Thus R. Bultmann, *Die Geschichte der synoptischen Tradition*, 4th

ed. (Göttingen, 1958), 285-87; idem, *Theologie des Neuen Testaments,* 6th ed. (Tübingen, 1968), 42f., 61f., 146ff., 314f.

3. It was above all J. Jeremias, *Die Abendmahlsworte Jesu,* 3rd ed. (Göttingen, 1960), who demonstrated the Jewish background, although he based his own interpretation too one-sidedly on the disputed hypothesis that the Last Supper was a Passover meal. See also Strack-Billerbeck IV, 74-76. On this question, see R. Feneberg, *Christliche Passafeier und Abendmahl: Eine biblisch-hermeneutische Untersuchung der neutestamentlichen Einsetzungsberichte,* StANT 27 (Munich, 1971). On the Old Testament background in general, an important essay is F. Hahn, "Die alttestamentlichen Motive in der urchristlichen Abendmahlsüberlieferung," *EvTh* 27 (1967): 337-74.

4. Cf. Strack-Billerbeck IV, 620f., 627ff.; J. Jeremias, *Die Abendmahlsworte Jesu,* 103ff.

5. This is emphasized above all by H. Schürmann, "Die Gestaltung der urchristlichen Eucharistiefeier," in idem, *Ursprung und Gestalt: Erörterungen und Besinnungen zum Neuen Testament* (Düsseldorf, 1970), 79ff.; idem, "Das Weiterleben der Sache Jesu im nachösterlichen Herrenmahl. Die Kontinuität der Zeichen in der Diskontinuität der Zeiten," in idem, *Jesu ureigener Tod: Exegetische Besinnungen und Ausblicke* (Freiburg, Basle, and Vienna, 1975), 76ff. The same position is taken by G. Delling, "Abendmahl II. Urchristliches Mahl-Verständnis," *Theologische Realenzyklopädie* (= *TRE*) I (1977): 49.

6. Thus J. Betz in *Mysterium Salutis* (= *MySal*) IV/2 (Einsiedeln, Zurich, and Cologne, 1973), 193ff.

7. H. Conzelmann, *Grundriss der Theologie des Neuen Testaments* (Munich, 1967), 76, has pointed out the hermeneutical circle which these words imply, as well as the limits to the possibility of

determining with precision the words Jesus himself used at the Last Supper. On a deeper level, of course, this hermeneutical circle must be understood against the background of Jesus' "handing-on of himself" in and through the "handing-on" (*traditio*) of the church, and it must be evaluated positively, in theological terms, in view of the fact that Christ and the church belong together.

8. A different position is taken by R. Pesch, who locates the narrative account in Mark within the life of Jesus, unlike the cultic aetiology presented by Paul, which has its *Sitz-im-Leben* in the earliest community: cf. *Das Markusevangelium*, HThK/NT (Freiburg, Basle, and Vienna, 1977), 2:354ff., and idem, *Wie Jesus das Abendmahl hielt: Der Grund der Eucharistie* (Freiburg, Basle, and Vienna, 1977), esp. 54. Against this, one must agree with other scholars, who object that Mark (with Matthew, who is dependent on the earliest Gospel) offers a text with a greater degree of liturgical stylization than Paul and Luke, since Mark and Matthew already draw together the logia over the bread and the cup, whereas these words are separated by the intervening meal in the accounts by Paul and Luke; cf., e.g., G. Bornkamm, "Herrenmahl und Kirche bei Paulus," in idem, *Studien zu Antike und Christentum, Gesammelte Aufsätze* 2 (Munich, 1959), 150ff.; H. Conzelmann, *Grundriss der Theologie des Neuen Testaments*, 74; G. Delling, "Abendmahl II," 48, 51, 54.

9. This continuity is set out in various ways by J. Betz, H. Schürmann, H. Patsch, G. Delling, and other scholars, who provide the detailed exegetical observations on which my remarks in this section are based.

10. On this, cf. K. Kertelge, ed., *Der Tod Jesu. Deutungen im*

Neuen Testament, Questiones disputatae (= QD) 74 (Freiburg, Basle, and Vienna, 1976).

11. Thus J. Ratzinger, *Eucharistie—Mitte der Kirche* (Munich, 1978), 10, 18.

12. Thus J. Betz, *MySal,* IV/2, 263f.

13. This is expressed very clearly in his *De captivitate Babylonica ecclesiae* (1520): WA 6:512-36.

14. We cannot discuss here the complicated individual exegetical questions about how Jesus understood "sacrifice." See n. 10 above and nn. 33f., as well as F. Hahn, "Das Verständnis des Opfers im Neuen Testament," in K. Lehmann and E. Schlink, eds., *Das Opfer Jesu Christi und seine Gegenwart in der Kirche: Klärungen zum Opfercharakter des Herrenmahles,* Dialog der Kirchen 3 (Freiburg i. Br. and Göttingen, 1983), 51-91.

15. For the first approach, see H. Küng, *Christ sein* (Munich, 1974), 312-15; for the second, see W. Marxsen, *Das Abendmahl als christologisches Problem* (Gütersloh, 1963).

16. See the overview in P. Neuenzeit, *Das Herrenmahl: Studien zur paulinischen Eucharistieauffassung,* StANT I (Munich, 1960), 136-47.

17. It was above all H. Lietzmann, *Messe und Herrenmahl: Eine Studie zur Geschichte der Liturgie,* Arbeiten zur Kirchengeschichte 8 (Bonn, 1926), who argued that the Eucharist was derived from the hellenistic meal in memory of the dead. The supposed provenance from the mystery religions played an important role in O. Casel's theology of the "mysteries," which is summed up in his book *Das christliche Kultmysterium,* 4th ed., revised and expanded, ed. B. Neunheuser (Regensburg, 1960). The background in the Old Testament and Judaism has been examined by J. Jeremias, *Die Abendmahlsworte Jesu,* 229-46; M. Thurian, *L'Eucharistie: Mémorial du*

Seigneur, sacrifice d'action de grâces et d'intercession (Neuchâtel and Paris, 1959); L. Bouyer, *Eucharistie: Théologie et spiritualité de la prière eucharistique* (Paris, 1966), 87f., 107f.

18. Strack-Billerbeck IV/I, 68.

19. Cf. J. Betz, *Die Eucharistie in der Zeit der griechischen Väter,* I/I (Freiburg i. Br., 1955), 197ff.; G. Kretschmar, "Abendmahl III/I. Alte Kirche," *TRE* I (1977): 62ff., 78ff. On the problem of hellenization which arises in this context, in the sense of a hermeneutically necessary translation, see ibid., 84-86.

20. Thomas Aquinas, *Summa theologiae* III q. 60 a. 3.

21. "The memorial of his passion is carried out, the mind is filled with grace, and a pledge of future glory is given us."

22. Cf. A. Gerken, *Theologie der Eucharistie* (Munich, 1973), 61ff., 97ff.

23. Cf. E. Iserloh, "Abendmahl III/2. Mittelalter," *TRE* I (1977): 100f., 128ff.

24. Cf. DH 1740.

25. In particular, we must refer here to P. Brunner, "Zur Lehre vom Gottesdienst der im Namen Jesu versammelten Gemeinde," *Leiturgia: Handbuch des evangelischen Gottesdienstes* I (Kassel, 1954), 209ff., 229ff.; J. J. von Allmen, *Ökumene im Herrenmahl* (Kassel, 1968), 25ff., 98ff.; and M. Thurian, *L'Eucharistie.* Cf. the overview in W. Averbeck, *Der Opfercharakter des Abendmahls in der neueren evangelischen Theologie,* KKTS 19 (Paderborn, 1967); U. Kühn, "Abendmahl IV. Das Abendmahlsgespräch in der ökumenischen Theologie der Gegenwart," *TRE* I (1977): 157ff., 164ff., 192ff.; K. Lehmann and E. Schlink, eds., *Das Opfer Jesu Christi und seine Gegenwart in der Kirche.*

26. Constitution on the liturgy, *Sacrosanctum Concilium* 6 and 47.

27. See H. Schlier, "Die Verkündigung im Gottesdienst der Kirche," in idem, *Die Zeit der Kirche: Exegetische Aufsätze und Vorträge,* 2nd ed. (Freiburg i. Br., 1958), 246ff.; K. Rahner, "Wort und Eucharistie," in idem, *Schriften zur Theologie* 4 (Einsiedeln, Zurich, and Cologne, 1960), 313-56, now available in K. Rahner, *Sämtliche Werke* 18 (Freiburg i. Br., 2003), 596-626.

28. We cannot speak in detail here of the various ways in which Jesus Christ is present in the Eucharist. See J. Betz, in *Die Eucharistie in der Zeit der griechischen Väter,* 267ff.; F. Eisenbach, *Die Gegenwart Jesu Christi im Gottesdienst: Systematische Studien zur Liturgiekonstitution des II. Vatikanischen Konzils* (Mainz, 1982). Still less can we discuss recent scholarly attempts to employ the terms transubstantiation, transignification, and transfinalization to reach a deeper understanding of the real presence; but see n. 77 below.

29. H. Beyer, *"eulogeō," Theologisches Wörterbuch zum Neuen Testament* (= *ThWNT*) 2:757ff.; H. Conzelmann, *"eucharisteō," ThWNT* 9:401ff.; L. Lies, *Wort und Eucharistie bei Origenes: Zur Spiritualisierungstendenz des Eucharistieverständnisses,* ITS 1 (Innsbruck, Vienna, and Munich, 1978), 11-36.

30. Ignatius of Antioch, *Letter to the Smyrnaeans* 8:1; *Letter to the Philadelphians* 4; Justin, *Dialogue with Trypho* 41; 117. Cf. J. A. Jungmann, "Von der 'Eucharistia' zur 'Messe,'" *Zeitschrift für katholische Theologie* (= *ZKTh*) 89 (1967): 29f.; H. Conzelmann, *"eucharisteō,"* 405.

31. J. A. Jungmann, *Missarum Solemnia: Eine genetische Erklärung der römischen Messe,* 5th ed. (Vienna, 1962), 1:20f., 38; 2:138ff.

32. Thus J. A. Jungmann, *Missarum Solemnia,* 1:27f.; J. Ratzinger, "Gestalt und Gehalt der eucharistischen Feier," in idem, *Das Fest des Glaubens* (Einsiedeln, 1981), 31-46. L. Bouyer

(*Eucharistie*) has made an impressive attempt to interpret the Eucharist in its totality on the basis of the aspect of *beraka*. For a summary and further comments, see K. Kues, *"Eulogia*. Überlegungen zur formalen Sinngestalt der Eucharistie," *ZKTh* 100 (1978): 69-97.

33. H. Gese, "Die Herkunft des Herrenmahls," in idem, *Zur biblischen Theologie* (Munich, 1977), 107-27; this idea is taken up by J. Ratzinger, "Gestalt und Gehalt der eucharistischen Feier," 47-54.

34. J. Betz, *Die Eucharistie in der Zeit der griechischen Väter*, II/I, 40.

35. J. A. Jungmann, *Missarum Solemnia*, I:31ff.; idem, "Von der 'Eucharistia' zur 'Messe,'" 29f.; H. Conzelmann, *"eucharisteō*," 405.

36. J. A. Jungmann, "Von der 'Eucharistia' zur 'Messe,'" 33. Cf. H. Moll, *Die Lehre von der Eucharistie als Opfer: Eine dogmengeschichtliche Untersuchung vom Neuen Testament bis Irenäus von Lyon*, Theophaneia 26 (Cologne and Bonn, 1975).

37. A decisive factor here was the fact that Isidore of Seville detached the preface—the prayer of thanksgiving in the narrower sense of the term—from the rest of the canon, thus dissolving the organic structure of the eucharistic anaphora. See J. R. Geiselmann, *Die Abendmahlslehre an der Wende der christlichen Spätantike zum Frühmittelalter: Isidor von Sevilla und das Sakrament der Eucharistie* (Munich, 1933).

38. *Apologia Confessionis Augustanae* 24 (BSLK 353ff.). Against this view, the Council of Trent maintains that the Eucharist is a genuine and specific sacrifice (DH 1751), not only an act of praise and thanksgiving but an expiatory sacrifice (DH 1753).

39. Cf. J. Ratzinger, "Ist die Eucharistie ein Opfer?," *Concilium* (German ed.) 3 (1967): 299-304, and n. 25 above.

40. Thus Augustine, *De civitate Dei* 10.20; 10.6. On this whole question, see H. U. von Balthasar, "Die Messe, ein Opfer der Kirche?," in idem, *Spiritus Creator*, Skizzen zur Theologie 3 (Einsiedeln, 1967), 166-217.

41. Cf. T. Schneider, *Zeichen der Nähe Gottes: Grundriss der Sakramententheologie* (Mainz, 1979), 144ff.

42. Irenaeus of Lyons, *Adversus Haereses* 4.19. The inherent unity of theocentricity and anthropocentricity is emphasized above all by E. Lengeling, who presents his arguments in "Liturgie," *Handbuch theologischer Grundbegriffe*, HThG, 2:81ff., 88ff.

43. H. Conzelmann, *"eucharisteō,"* 403.

44. On the meaning of the epiclesis, see O. Casel, "Zur Epiklese," *Jahrb. Lit.* 3 (1923): 100-102; idem, "Neue Beiträge zur Epiklesefrage," *Jahrb. Lit.* 4 (1924): 169-78; J. A. Jungmann, *Missarum Solemnia*, 2:238ff.; J. Betz, *Die Eucharistie in der Zeit der griechischen Väter*, I/I, 320-46; J. P. de Jong, "Epiklese," *LThK*, 2nd ed. III, cols. 935-37.

45. Thus J. Betz, *Die Eucharistie in der Zeit der griechischen Väter*, 319.

46. H. Beyer, *"eulogeō,"* 752ff.; L. Lies, *Wort und Eucharistie*, 61f.

47. J. A. Jungmann, "Von der 'Eucharistia' zur 'Messe,'" 37. We already find this meaning of the noun in Origen, though of course still embedded in the larger holistic context. Cf. L. Lies, *Wort und Eucharistie*, 261ff., 294ff.

48. J. A. Jungmann, "Von der 'Eucharistia' zur 'Messe,'" 38; idem, "Zur Bedeutungsgeschichte des Wortes 'Missa,'" in idem, *Gewordene Liturgie* (Innsbruck and Leipzig, 1941), 34-52; for other interpretations, see J. J. von Allmen, *Ökumene im Herrenmahl*, 120f.

49. J. A. Jungmann, "Von der 'Eucharistia' zur 'Messe,'" 39.

50. This applies especially to the Lima declaration on "Bap-

tism, Eucharist, and Ministry" (1982); cf. U. Kühn, "Abendmahl IV," 197.

51. This has been particularly emphasized by E. Käsemann, "Anliegen und Eigenart der paulinischen Abendmahlslehre," in idem, *Exegetische Versuche und Besinnungen* (Göttingen, 1960), I:11-33; cf. P. Neuenzeit, *Das Herrenmahl*, 48f., 185f.

52. H. R. Schlette, *Kommunikation und Sakrament*, QD 8 (Freiburg, Basle, and Vienna, 1960).

53. J. Betz, *Die Eucharistie in der Zeit der griechischen Väter*, 328ff.

54. See, e.g., J. Meyendorff, "Zum Eucharistieverständnis der orthodoxen Kirche," *Concilium* (German ed.) 3 (1967): 291-94.

55. See J. J. von Allmen, *Ökumene im Herrenmahl*, 32ff.

56. O. Casel, "Die Logiké thysia der antiken Mystik in christlich-liturgischer Umdeutung," *JLW* 4 (1924): 37-47.

57. F. Hauck, *"koinōnos," ThWNT* 3:798-810; P. C. Bori, *Koinōnia. L'idea della comunione nell'ecclesiologia recente e il Nuovo Testamento* (Brescia, 1972).

58. Augustine, *Commentary on John* 26.6 and 13. This affirmation has played an important role over many centuries in the documents of the ecclesiastical magisterium: DH 802; 1635; UR 47.

59. R. Guardini, *Besinnung vor der Feier der Heiligen Messe*, part 2, 2nd ed. (Mainz, 1939), 73ff.; it was, of course, not Guardini's intention to offer a definition of the essence of the Eucharist (cf. 75), still less to call into question the sacrificial character as the source and presupposition of the Eucharist (cf. 77). A similar position is taken by J. Pascher, *Eucharistia: Gestalt und Vollzug* (Münster, 1947); idem, "Um die Grundgestalt der Eucharistie," *Münchner Theologische Zeitschrift* (= *MThZ*) 1 (1950): 64-75. On the theological debate at that period, see T. Maas-Eward, *Die Krise der*

Liturgischen Bewegung in Deutschland und Österreich. Zu den Auseinander-
setzungen um die "liturgische Frage" in den Jahren 1939 bis 1944, StPLi 3
(Regensburg, 1981), esp. 343-48. For the more recent discussion, see n. 32 above.

60. On this, see the important essay by H. Schürmann that
has been cited several times above, "Die Gestalt der urchristlichen
Eucharistiefeier."

61. We see this in the well-known letter sent by Pliny to Tra-
jan (10.9) and in Justin, *First Apology* 67.

62. J. A. Jungmann, "'Abendmahl' als Name der Eucharistie,"
ZKTh 93 (1971): 91-94.

63. Cf. P. Neuenzeit, *Das Herrenmahl,* 191ff.; F. Lang,
"Abendmahl und Bundesgedanke im Neuen Testament," *EvTh* 35
(1975): 524-38; V. Wagner, "Die Bedeutungswandel von berit
hadascha bei der Ausgestaltung der Abendmahlsworte," *EvTh* 35
(1975): 538-52.

64. Cf. P. Neuenzeit, *Das Herrenmahl,* 201-19; E. Schweizer,
"*sōma,*" *ThWNT* 7:1065f.; E. Käsemann, "Das theologische Problem des Motivs vom Leibe Christi," in idem, *Paulinische Perspektiven*
(Tübingen, 1969), 178-210.

65. Augustine, *Sermon* 272.

66. Cf. above all Henri de Lubac, *Corpus mysticum: L'Eucharistie*
et l'Église au Moyen Age (Paris, 1944). His position is followed by A.
Gerken, *Theologie der Eucharistie,* 122ff.

67. Thomas Aquinas, *Summa theologiae* III q. 73 ad 6: "We can
consider three things in this sacrament: viz. its aspect as sacrament alone, viz. bread and wine; and its aspect as reality and
sacrament, viz. the true body of Christ; and its aspect as reality
alone, viz. the effect(s) of this sacrament" (*in hoc sacramento tria con-*
siderare possumus: scilicet id quod est sacramentum tantum, scilicet panis et

vinum; et id quod est res et sacramentum, scilicet corpus Christi verum; et id quod est res tantum, scilicet effectus huius sacramenti); q. 80 a. 4: "The reality of this sacrament is twofold . . . the first, that which is signified and contained, viz. Christ himself; the second is signified and not contained, viz. the mystical body of Christ, which is the fellowship of the saints (*duplex autem est res huius sacramenti . . . una quidem quae est significata et contenta, scilicet ipse Christus; alia autem est significata et non contenta, scilicet corpus Christi mysticum, quod est societas sanctorum*): cf. q. 60 a. 3 *sed contra*; q. 73 a. 2 *sed contra.*

68. SC 11, 14, 48. This renewed understanding of the link between Eucharist and church has had important consequences for a eucharistic ecclesiology which takes its starting point not in the universal church but in the local church which celebrates the Eucharist, understanding the unity of the universal church as the *communio* of the local churches.

69. Cf. K. Lehmann, "Persönliches Gebet in der Eucharistiefeier," *IKaZ Communio* (1977): 401-6. Space does not allow me to discuss the important topic of eucharistic adoration and veneration outside the celebration of the Mass.

70. On the question of a new *disciplina arcani*, see H. Spaemann, *Und Gott schied das Licht von der Finsternis: Christliche Konsequenzen* (Freiburg, Basle, and Vienna, 1982), 93-140.

71. This is the position of J. Moltmann, *Kirche in der Kraft des Geistes: Ein Beitrag zur messianischen Ekklesiologie* (Munich, 1975), 272f., 285f.

72. "Likewise, in the sacrament of the eucharistic bread, the unity of believers, who form one body in Christ (cf. 1 Cor 10:17), is both expressed and brought about" (LG 3). "Then, strengthened by the body of Christ in the eucharistic communion, the faithful manifest in a concrete way that unity of the

People of God which this holy sacrament aptly signifies and admirably realizes" (LG 11).

73. According to Catholic doctrine, the Eucharist presupposes a validly ordained minister: cf. DH 802; 1752; LG 26, 28; UR 22. On this doctrinal question, cf. P. Bläser et al., *Amt und Eucharistie*, KKSMI 10 (Paderborn, 1973). Another view is taken by H. Küng, *Wozu Priester?* (Zurich, Einsiedeln, and Cologne, 1971); E. Schillebeeckx, *Das kirchliche Amt* (Düsseldorf, 1981).

74. On this, see the overview by G. Wingren, "Abendmahl V. Das Abendmahl als Tischgemeinschaft nach ethischen Gesichtspunkten," *TRE* I (1977): 212-29.

75. Cf. G. Wainwright, *Eucharist and Eschatology* (New York, 1981).

76. Thus K. Kues, *Eulogia*, 94-97, building on the work by J. A. Jungmann and J. Ratzinger. Cf. n. 32 above.

77. Thus J. Betz, *MySal* IV/2, 264f. For the corresponding interpretation of the doctrine of transubstantiation, cf. J. Ratzinger, "Das Problem der Transsubstantiation und die Frage nach dem Sinn der Eucharistie," *ThQ* 147 (1967): esp. 152f.

Chapter 6: Eucharist: Sacrament of Unity

1. J. Lécuyer, "Die liturgische Versammlung. Biblische und patristische Grundlagen," *Concilium* (German ed.) 2 (1966): 79-87. This aspect has been strongly underlined by A. Schmemann, *The Eucharist: Sacrament of the Kingdom* (New York, 2003), 11-26. His polemic against Western theology is justified, as far as the traditional theology of the handbooks is concerned, but does not begin to do justice to the great scholastic theology.

2. W. Bauer, *Wörterbuch zum Neuen Testament* (Berlin, 1958), 477f.

3. Augustine, *Commentary on John* 26.6, 13.

4. DH 802.

5. Decree on the Sacrament of the Eucharist (DH 1635).

6. Thomas Aquinas, *Summa theologiae* III 73, 6.

7. *Summa theologiae* III 73, 5.

8. *Summa theologiae* III 73, 3; cf. IV *Sent.* D. 45 q. 2 a, 3 qa I c.

9. Bonaventure, *Sent.* IV d.8, p.2, a. 2 q. I; Thomas Aquinas, *Summa theologiae* III 73, 6.

10. Freely translated: "to say that something exists, is the same thing as saying that it is one." See the overview by P. Hadot and K. Flasch, "Eine (das), Einheit," *HWPh* 2 (1972): 361-77.

11. On the *exitus-reditus* motif, cf. M. Seckler, *Das Heil in der Geschichte: Geschichtstheologisches Denken bei Thomas von Aquin* (Munich, 1964).

12. W. Welsch, *Unsere postmoderne Moderne* (Weinheim, 1987).

13. E. Käsemann, *Exegetische Versuche und Besinnungen* (Göttingen, 1960), 1:214-23; (Göttingen, 1964), 2:262-67. His point of reference here is the variety of ecclesiological conceptions in the New Testament. We cannot dispute the existence of this pluralism, but we must ask whether it is methodologically acceptable to place differences in the first century on the same level as the confessional divergences that emerged from the sixteenth century onward under completely new historical presuppositions. The formation of confessional churches is a historical phenomenon that became possible only under the specific conditions of the Reformation and of the early modern period. Furthermore, this line of argument overlooks the fact that we can already see in the

New Testament—especially in the Acts of the Apostles and in the Pastoral Letters—the development from the apostolic to our own postapostolic age. This makes it problematic to give preference to the earliest strata and documents. Ultimately, it was the church of the second and third centuries, with its episcopal constitution, that collected the various New Testament documents together into one single canon, thereby also giving what Käsemann identifies as a charismatically orientated ecclesiology an abiding "residence permit" in the episcopally structured church.

14. H. de Lubac, "Pluralismus oder Harmonie?" in *Quellen kirchlicher Einheit* (Einsiedeln, 1974), 55-66.

15. Cf. also Matt 8:11; Mark 13:27; John 11:51f.; *Didache* 10:5; *1 Clement* 29:1-30; 59:3f.

16. W. Kasper, *Jesus der Christus* (Mainz, 1974), 83-103.

17. According to Y. Spiteris, *Ecclesiologia ortodossa* (Bologna, 2003), there are two tendencies in contemporary Orthodox ecclesiology. The one tends to see the church and the liturgy from a protological point of view, as the icon of the preexistent heavenly church (I. Karmiris), while the other tendency considers the church as the earthly icon of the eschatological heavenly church (J. Zizioulas). Both tendencies emphasize in various ways the importance of the universal cosmic dimension.

18. J. Ratzinger, *Der Geist der Liturgie* (Freiburg i. Br., 2000), 20-29.

19. Eng. tr.: "The Mass on the World," in *The Heart of Matter* (New York: HarperCollins, 1978), 119ff.

20. G. von Rad, *Theologie des Alten Testaments* (Munich, 1969), I:275-85. On the general phenomenological and hermeneutical context, see P. Ricoeur, *Symbolism of Evil* (Boston, 1969). On the theological interpretation, see W. Kasper, *Jesus der Christus* (Mainz, 1974), 140-44, 254-69.

21. The theory of "satisfaction" proposed by Anselm of Canterbury has often been harshly criticized, but it should be understood in this sense. The intention is not to appease the wrath of God and satisfy his desire for revenge; rather, this theory wishes to affirm that the order of things, which had been disturbed, is now reestablished, so that a new order of peace and of reconciliation is begun.

22. This truth had been forgotten for a long time, but we have become newly conscious of it, thanks to B. Poschmann, Karl Rahner, and other scholars working in the spirit of the early church.

23. UR 6f.; encyclical *Ut unum sint* 15f.; 21; 30; 34f.

24. D. Bonhoeffer, *Nachfolge* (Munich, 1971), 13f. (Eng. trans., Brian McNeil).

25. A. von Harnack, *Das Wesen des Christentums,* Gütersloher Taschenbücher 227 (Gütersloh, 1977), 43 (Eng. trans., Brian McNeil).

26. Ignatius, *Letter to the Ephesians* 5.2f.; 13.1; *Letter to the Philadelphians* 6.2; *Letter to the Magnesians* 7.1f. For further textual references, see J. Lécuyer, "Die liturgische Versammlung," 83.

27. On the interpretation of these texts, drawing on a wide range of scholarly discussions, see W. Schrage, *Der erste Brief an die Korinther,* EKK VII/2 (Solothurn and Neukirchen, 1995), 430-42.

28. Cyprian, *Ep.* 69.5, 3; Augustine, *Sermons* 272 and 234a. Many texts are presented by H. de Lubac, *Katholizismus als Gemeinschaft* (Einsiedeln, 1943), 79-99.

29. Augustine, *Commentary on John* 26.6, 13; Thomas Aquinas, *Summa theologiae* III 73, 6. For the documents of the Second Vatican Council, see SC 47; LG 3; 7; and so forth.

30. Augustine, *Contra Faustum* 12.20; *Sermon* 57.7.

31. *Sermon* 63.7; quoted in LG 26.

32. H. de Lubac, *Corpus mysticum. L'Eucharistie et l'Église au Moyen Age,* 2nd ed. (Paris, 1949).

33. Martin Luther, *Ein Sermon von dem hochwürdigen Sakrament des heiligen wahren Leichnams Christi und von den Bruderschaften,* WA 2:742-45.

34. H. de Lubac, *Betrachtung über die Kirche* (Graz, 1954), 97-106.

35. "The sacrament of sacraments": *Suppl.* 7.2.

36. LG 11; CD 30; PO 5.

37. Thomas Aquinas, *Summa theologiae* III 83,4.

38. LG 3; 7; 11; 17; 26; UR 2; 15; CD 30.

39. H. de Lubac, "Einzelkirche und Ortskirche," in *Quellen kirchlicher Einheit,* 43-54.

40. The basic works here are L. Hertling, *Communio und Primat* (Rome, 1943); W. Elert, *Abendmahl und Kirchen-Gemeinschaft* (Berlin, 1954). The most important Orthodox authors are A. Afanasiev, J. Meyendorff, A. Schmemann, and J. Zizioulas; the most important Catholic authors are H. de Lubac, Y. Congar, J. Hamer, M. J. Le Guillou, J. M. R. Tillard, P. Fransen, J. Ratzinger, O. Saier, E. Corecco, P. W. Scheele, W. Kasper, M. Kehl, B. Forte, G. Greshake, and J. Hilberath.

41. Y. Congar, "De la communion des Églises à une ecclésiologie universelle," in *L'épiscopat et l'Église universelle* (Paris, 1962), 227-60.

42. SC 26; LG 23; CD 11.

43. Meyer-Strathmann, *"leitourgeō,"* *ThWNT* 4:221-39; P. G. Müller, "Kollekte I," *LThK,* 3rd ed., 6 (1997): 181.

44. L. Bouyer, *Die Kirche* (Einsiedeln, 1977), I:33f.

45. John Paul II, *Ut unum sint* 9.

46. *Ut unum sint* 9; 20.

47. *Ut unum sint* 7.

48. Canon 844; Directory for the Practice of the Principles and Norms in Ecumenical Work (1993), 130f.; instruction *Redemptoris sacramentum* 84.

49. John Paul II, *Ut unum sint* 46; *Ecclesia de eucharistia* 46.

50. For Thomas Aquinas, this is the meaning of *epikeia* as the higher justice: cf. *Summa theologiae* II/II q. 120.

51. LG 8; UR 4; *Ut unum sint* 10.

52. Irenaeus of Lyons, *Adversus haereses* 3.24.1.

53. John Paul II, *Ut unum sint* 18.

54. *Ut unum sint* 34.

55. *Ut unum sint* 28; 57.

56. J. Ratzinger, "Eucaristia e missione," in *La comunione nella Chiesa* (Milan, 2004), 93-128.

57. Y. Congar, *Diversités et communion* (Paris, 1982), 243f.

58. John Paul II, *Ut unum sint* 5.

Indexes

Biblical Texts

Authors and Persons

Walter Cardinal Kasper

A Short Biography

Walter Cardinal Kasper was born on March 5, 1933. He was ordained priest in the cathedral of Rottenburg on April 6, 1957. He was appointed professor of dogmatic theology at the University of Münster in 1964 and professor of dogmatic theology at the University of Tübingen in 1970. He collaborated at the Synod of the German dioceses in Würzburg from 1972 to 1975. In 1979, he was appointed consultor of the Pontifical Council for the Promotion of Christian Unity and representative of the Catholic Church in the Commission for Faith and Order of the World Council of Churches. He was the principal author of the first volume of the German adult catechism, published in 1985 (Eng. trans.: *The Church's Confession of Faith*).

He was bishop of Rottenburg-Stuttgart from 1989 to 1999. In the latter year, he was appointed secretary of the Pontifical Council for the Promotion of Christian Unity and vice-president of the Pontifical Commission for Religious Relations with Judaism. He was created cardinal in 2001 and appointed president of both these Vatican bodies. He is a member of the

Congregations for the Doctrine of the Faith and for the Eastern Catholic Churches.

Cardinal Kasper has received numerous honorary doctorates. He is honorary professor at the University of Tübingen, and a member of the Heidelberg Academy of Sciences and of the European Academy of Sciences and Arts. He has been awarded the Cross of Merit (1st Class) of the German Federal Republic (1987), the Medal of Merit of the Federal State of Baden-Württemberg (1998), the St. Boniface Medal of the German Episcopal Conference (1999), and the Great Order of Merit with Star and Sash of the Federal Republic of Germany (2004).

His most important publications include *Der Gott Jesu Christi* (Eng. trans.: *The God of Jesus Christ*); *Jesus, der Christus* (Eng. trans.: *Jesus the Christ*); *Einführung in den Glauben: Theologie und Kirche* (2 vols.; Eng. trans. of vol. I: *Theology and Church*; some essays from the second volume in *Leadership in the Church*).

He is editor-in-chief of the *Lexikon für Theologie und Kirche*.